COUNTRYMAN ON THE MOORS

John C. Atkinson

Countryman on the Moors

EDITED BY
JOHN G. O'LEARY

Oxford   New York
OXFORD UNIVERSITY PRESS
1983

Oxford University Press, Walton Street, Oxford OX2 6DP

London Glasgow New York Toronto
Delhi Bombay Calcutta Madras Karachi
Kuala Lumpur Singapore Hong Kong Tokyo
Nairobi Dar es Salaam Cape Town
Melbourne Auckland
and associated companies in
Beirut Berlin Ibadan Mexico City Nicosia

Oxford is a trade mark of Oxford University Press

British Library Cataloguing in Publication Data
Atkinson, John C.
(Forty years in a moorland parish).
Countryman on the moors. – (Oxford paperbacks)
1. Scarborough (North Yorkshire) – Description
I. Title II. Countryman on the moors
III. O'Leary, John G.
914.28'470481 DA690.528
ISBN 0-19-281414-1

Library of Congress Cataloging in Publication Data
Atkinson, J. C. (John Christopher), 1814 – 1900.
Countryman on the moors.
(Oxford paperbacks)
Selections from Forty years in a moorland parish.
1. Cleveland – Social life and customs. 2. Folklore – England – Cleveland.
3. Cleveland – Antiquities. 4. England – Antiquities.
5. Atkinson, J. C. (John Christopher), 1814 – 1900.
I. O'Leary, John Gerard. II. Title.
DA670.C63A8 1983 942.8'5081 83-8025
ISBN 0-19-281414-1 (pbk.)

Printed in Great Britain by
Richard Clay (The Chaucer Press) Ltd.
Bungay, Suffolk

CONTENTS

INTRODUCTION   *page* 7

1 DANBY IN 1850   11

2 HOB AT WORK   29

3 WITCH WORK   41

4 THE WISE MAN   52

5 DIGGING UP THE PAST   71

6 ANCIENT BRITAIN   90

7 HILLS AND DALES   103

8 GRAVES ANCIENT AND RECENT   113

9 DOGS IN CHURCH   123

10 WINTER ON THE MOORS   137

INTRODUCTION

THIS BOOK was first published in 1891 under the title of *Forty Years in a Moorland Parish*: the present edition is selected from the original, a work of very considerable length, and I have left out a great deal of local history and archaeology which does not match up to modern requirements on these subjects. I have endeavoured, though, to leave untouched the author's valuable account of the North Riding of Yorkshire in the second half of the last century.

John Christopher Atkinson was born in 1814 at Goldhanger in Essex where his father was curate: he went to school at Kelvedon and later entered St John's, Cambridge, as a sizar, eventually taking his degree: he became ordained in 1842. He arrived at Danby in the North Riding in 1850 at the age of thirty-six and died at the same place, having led to the altar three wives by whom he had thirteen children.

His published works deal with a wide variety of interests, and all show that love of nature which his remote parish in the midst of wild moorland served so well. While taking his duties as a parson seriously, he meanwhile pursued his studies and archaeological speculations, as well as recording endless talks with old Yorkshire men and women who had never set foot outside the dales. He died on the 31st of March 1900 at the age of eighty-six, with a full and satisfied mind.

JOHN GERARD O'LEARY

Countryman on the Moors

CHAPTER ONE

Danby in 1850

THE way in which I came to find myself planted in Danby was as follows. A letter, written with the intention that it should be read by me, in which this parish, with its ecclesiastical income of £95 a year, was described as one affording a fine field for work to any one so inclined. There was a church in it, it was true, but distant from the over-whelming majority of the parishioners – exceeding 1500 in number – by from one and a quarter to four miles, upwards even of that in some directions. There was a clergyman, too, but he had not been famed for strength of body nor energy of mind and purpose; so that, while there were Wesleyan Methodists and Primitive Methodists, in numbers and organization alike considerable, Churchmen were not conspicuous in either the one respect or the other; a condition of matters which of course need occasion no surprise under the circumstances. But even this was not all; for when I mentioned to a shipowning friend, who had been a seafaring man in his earlier days, that I had thoughts of going a-prospecting, and looking at the place, in consideration of the offer of the living made to me, his view of my wisdom, and of the eligibility of the place itself, was expressed as follows: 'Going to see yon place! Why, Danby was not found out when they sent Bonaparte to St Helena; or else they never would have taken the trouble to send him all the way there!'

However, I had my own reasons; and one fine afternoon, six-and-forty years ago, I found myself riding along the not too traffic-worn road to Whitby from Scarborough. Born and reared a South-country-man, and not as yet conversant with the wild solitary tracks and the deep pitches and steep ravine-banks of the North Yorkshire moors, I was but little prepared for some of the sights and sounds that greeted my unaccustomed perceptions. One might sometimes see an eagle in those days still;[1] and two or three large hawks might well be seen on

[1] Footnote on following page.

the wing at once; and the curlew skirled as he crossed, far above your head, from the wild moors of Goathland or Glaisdale, where he bred then and breeds still, to the sea-coast on the east. Hitherto, moreover, I had been accustomed to regard the sheep as a quiet, unimpulsive sort of creature, with unstartling habits, much given to the pursuits of growing wool and developing the masses of fat not loved by boys at school; but during the experiences of this ride my preconceived notions were exposed to a very rude shock. For I saw a sheep – there could be no doubt that it *was* a sheep – deliberately, – no, I must not use that word, for there was no deliberation about the act, – I saw it jauntily skip up a six-foot-high bank, steep as a wallside, and rugged with rock and brier, which rose from the road I was riding along to the foot of a five-foot-high rough mortarless stone wall or dike, and proceed incontinently to leap up part of the height and scramble the rest with cat-like activity and hoofs that clung like claws, and disappear in the enclosure on the other side. Other denizens of the moor too, besides these athletes among sheep, were there, and were noted by me as creatures to be much observed. For grouse and golden plover – a good pack of the one, or a large flock of the other – claimed my attention; or a series of symmetrical mounds, dotting the moor on either side of me – the intent and contents of which have been familiar enough to me since – were like the 'little star' to the child, and made me 'wonder what they were'.

Three hours' riding brought me to Whitby, and the quaint, picturesque old town – there were no lodging-houses there then; the Royal Hotel itself was not so much as projected – with the setting autumn sun gilding and glorifying its red roofs and quaint gables, impressed an image on my retina which has never faded away, and which has stirred the eye and the heart of many a one besides the artist with a longing for some lasting memento of its beauty.

The following morning saw me still farther on my journey of exploration. I was told I should find but few on the road to make

---

[1] On one occasion, not so very long after the date of the ride mentioned in the text, I saw, from near the eminence called Danby Beacon, an eagle on the wing, which doubtless was the bird which was taken or shot – I forget which – some few days after, at no great distance away, with a rabbit-trap attached to one of its feet. This was an erne or white-tailed eagle, from which the Arncliff of the West Arncliff woods in Egton parish, and the Arncliff of Ingleby Arncliff in West Cleveland, had both taken their names in the old Anglian times. On the same day, and in the same part of the moor, I saw a pair of hen harriers, and another large hawk, which might have been a buzzard, but was too far off to be identified. Once too I have seen the kite here; and in the older days ravens used to breed in the parish, and might be seen or heard any day, or almost every day.

inquiry of as to the route I was bound to pursue. After the first three or four miles, a rough moorland road would have to be traversed, and I might not see a passenger for miles and miles together. Nor did I. The heights of Swart Houe once attained, with the bare moor on either side of me, I passed on to Barton Howl without seeing a soul. Thence to Stonegate, according to the directions obtained at the little roadside inn just passed, and there the solitude of my way was singularly broken. I was no longer the sole traveller on this rugged lonely roadway; for there was a cavalcade such as I had never before imagined, much less realized. What I met was a stone-waggon with a team – a 'draught' we call it in our North Yorkshire vernacular – of no less than twenty horses and oxen attached to it, half of either kind. They were drawing a huge block of fine freestone up the terribly steep 'bank', or hill-side road, which rises like a house-roof on the eastern side of Stonegate Gill. At the foot of the bank, on the limited level space available, there were standing four other waggons similarly loaded. The full complement of animals dragging each of these 'carries' was a pair of horses and a yoke of oxen; and when they reached the foot of one of these stupendous hills, the full force of animal power was attached to each of the carriages in succession, and so the ponderous loads – five tons' weight on the average – were hauled to the top; and then, when all were up, the cavalcade proceeded on its slow march again. I had seen oxen used in the plough in Suffolk, but never before had I seen such a spectacle as this on the highroads of England.

At last I reached the Beacon, the highest point, houe-crowned, of all that part of the North Yorkshire moors, and the site of a beacon in Armada times, and on many subsequent occasions when it was thought or feared that invasion might ensue. Before me, looking westward, was moor, so that I could see nothing else. On either side was moor, with a valley on the left, and on the right, to the north, an expanse of cultivated land beyond. Across the valley just named there was moor again; and the valley was, it was clear, but a narrow one; while behind me, as I knew, lay three good miles of moor, and nothing but moor. It was a solitude, and a singularly lonely solitude. The only signs of life were given by the grouse, or the half-wild moor-sheep, whose fleeces here and there flecked the brown moor with white spots. It was a wild as well as a lonely solitude; and yet not dreary, nor could one well feel altogether alone. For there, from the south-east round by the north to Tees mouth on the north-east, and thence on again straight

out to the north along the coast of Durham and Northumberland, was
the great wide open sea; and no one feels alone in sight of the sea, any
more than under the clear canopy of a starry heaven in a bright cloud-
less winter's night. Nay, the stillness of such a night, far more than the
wild wailings of the rushing blast, is instinct with the wisht, weird
creatures of the imagination; far too much so for the superstitious or
fancy-led to be able to feel themselves alone; and more so yet to one
fairly cognisant of his inner life and its connections. And the sea, even
at a distance, is a creature – a being – full of a great vitality, and with
many voices; and by aid of one of them at least, whatever the mood of
the listener, there is an inner and most real communion with the unseen.

But I was at the Beacon, and with a choice of roads – at least of
tracks – before me; and beyond a general idea that I was too much to the
north to be in the right way, I had nothing to guide me. A direction-
post there was, but the arms which had once borne the names of the
places the various tracks led to were gone. There was nothing in sight
but moor, to the west, and to the north and south of the same; while
the track or rough road that appeared to lead downwards towards
the farther part, if not the termination, of the valley on my left, was
grass-grown and little used. My suspense and uncertainty were terminated in an unforeseen way. A woman, riding a strong pony, had come
up unseen and unheard behind me, the hoofs of her steed giving out no
sound on the grassy sward at the edge of the road. I asked her the way
to Danby; but whether she misunderstood my Southern English, or I
misunderstood her Yorkshire vernacular – a mighty easy thing to
happen, as I knew right well before long – or whether she did not like
the look of me, and preferred solitariness to company – for she was
herself bound for Danby Dale-end – the direction I took led me away
from the place I wished to reach, instead of directly towards it. A mile
and a half more of nothing but heather – or, in Yorkshire speech, 'ling'
– convinced me of what I had suspected before, namely, that I was too
far to the north, and now too far to the west, to be right for Danby
Dale. So the first road I came to bearing south was taken, and a mile
ridden along it brought me in sight of one of the loveliest scenes it had
ever been my lot to behold. There was the long valley, running east
and west, which had seemed to narrow when beheld from the grudging
heights above, and which was now seen to be from a mile to a mile and
a half broad, and with dale after dale, not wide but long and deep,
opening into it from its southern side. High on either side of each of

these dales towered the moorland banks, and along each dale I could trace the course of a minor stream, with its fringe of trees, running its descending race towards the main stream in the longer or medial valley. There was verdure everywhere, with plentiful signs of careful tillage, and the luxuriant growth springing from a grateful soil. It might be that, having had the wild wilderness of the brown moor around me for so long, the eye was doubly grateful for the fresh greens of the beck-side pastures and the widely-spread green crops. But with colour, contrast, and contour, soaring hill and deepening dale, abrupt nab-end and craggy wood, all claiming notice at once, rather than in their proper turn, the scene spread before me was something more than simply beautiful.

Ten minutes now brought me to a little country hostel, as clean as it was plain and unpretending, kept by two sisters known far and wide as 'Martha and Mary', and wherein, some two or three years after, I heard propounded the doughty question, 'Gin Adam had na sinned, how wad it ha' stooden then?' – and commending my horse to the care of the blacksmith, who officiated as ostler, I betook myself to a hamlet half a mile distant, where I was told I should find the 'minister'. The house I was told to look for was found without difficulty, but to find the 'minister' in it did not seem quite so easy. It was a long low gray build-ing, on a sort of grassy terrace by the roadside, and with nothing be-tween it and the roadway. At one end were a cow-house and other like premises, and at the other a low lean-to shed appearing to give access to some sort of a back-kitchen or scullery. Beyond the one window which looked out upon the highway was a door, twin to the one opening into the cow-house, and quite innocent of any such appendage as a knocker or a bell – innocent even, one would have said, of any nascent suspicion that such things existed. But seeing no other door and no way that seemed to lead to any other I made up my mind to knock at this one. I knocked once, twice and again, with no response. I learned in after days that I ought to have gone to the door in the lean-to, the only one in use by all the members of the family; for there in the kitchen, which was also the living-room, as it presently appeared, I should have found father and mother, son and four daughters, who, together with the daytal-man[1] (who was working for the father, and with the son), were just sitting down to dinner. Not suspecting this, I went on knocking;

[1] That is, a day-labourer; a man reckoned with by the day, in contra-distinction to one reckoned with by the term; a man the 'tale' of whose wages, or work, is from day to day.

and at last I heard a slow step evidently sounding from an uncarpeted floor of stone approaching the door. Slowly the door was unlocked and the bolts drawn, and as slowly was it opened; but not for more than a few inches. As well as I could see, the person who opened it was an old man, clad in a rusty black coat, with drab breeches and continuations, and with a volume of what was supposed to be white neckcloth about his throat. I asked, 'Does Mr D— live here?' and the answer was, 'Mr D— does live here.' I rejoined, 'Can I see Mr D—?' I was asked in return, 'What do you want with Mr D—?' – 'Well,' I said, naming the patron of the living, 'Lord Downe asked me to call on Mr D—.' My interlocutor responded, 'Lord Downe sent you to call on Mr D—! Why, last week he sent a Fowler Jones to call on Mr D—.' My reply was, 'I am not Mr Fowler Jones; my name is so-and-so. And Lord Downe told me he had written to Mr D—, mentioning my name, and not without reference to helping him in the parish. Can I see Mr D—?' – 'Why, yes, I suppose you can. I's Mr D—.' After this the door was opened a little more widely, and I was requested to walk in and partake of what I afterwards found was the dinner prepared for the family at large, who were meantime left hungry and expectant in the kitchen without.

In due time I was asked, Would I like to go and see the church? – a proposition to which I gave a willing assent. After a walk of a mile and a half it was reached, the door unlocked, and we entered. There is no need to dwell on what I saw of the condition of the said edifice. It must suffice to say that my conductor, the 'minister', entered without removing his hat, walked through the sacred building and up to the holy table with his hat still on. Although I had seen many an uncared-for church, and many a shabby altar, I thought I had reached the farthest extreme now. The altar-table was not only rickety, and with one leg shorter than the others, and besides that, mean and worm-eaten, but it was covered with what it would have been a severe and sarcastic libel to call a piece of green baize; for it was in rags, and of any or almost every colour save the original green. And even that was not all! It was covered thickly over with stale crumbs. It seemed impossible not to crave some explanation of this; and the answer to my inquiry was as nearly as possible in the following terms: 'Why, it is the Sunday School teachers. They must get their meat somewhere, and they gets it here.' It may be thought I am romancing, drawing upon my imagination. But indeed I am not; I am but detailing the literal fact. And everything was in hateful harmony with what I have thus described. There lay the dirty shabby surplice, flung negligently over the altar-railing, itself paintless and broken, and the vestment with half its length trailing on the dirty, unswept floor. The pulpit inside was reeking with accumulated dust and scraps of torn paper. The font was an elongated, attenuated reproduction of a double egg-cup, or hour-glass without the sustaining framework; and in it was a paltry slop-basin, lined with dust, and an end or two of tallow candle beside it.

Such was the parish church and its reverend but hardly reverent minister. And he was but one of a pair; for his brother was parish clerk and parish schoolmaster as well; and the first time I had to take a funeral, on arriving at the church a little in advance of the hour fixed, and entering the basement of the tower (which in the days of the barbarous re-edifying of the poor old church had been made to subserve the purposes of a porch), I became aware of a strong perfume of tobacco smoke; and there inside the church I saw the clerk sitting in the sunny embrasure of the west window, with his hat on of course, and comfortably smoking his pipe. A good harmless man enough, but one who might as happily be described by the effective Scottish word 'feckless' as by any more laboured attempt to convey an idea of him. He had begun his independent life not so ill provided for as a Dalesman of those days. His elder brother had had a university education, and he himself had received the patrimonial land, subject, I daresay, to some small burden on a sister's account. He had muddled through this in some way or other, but nobody knew how, and he himself least of all. He had smoked his pipe and played his 'cello, and I suppose done nothing much besides. And then, when at the end of his resources, mental and other, he had had the parish honours above named almost literally 'thrust upon him'. For, a little later in the course of my connection with the parish, I asked the worthy old gentleman who was then the senior church-warden, why this very incompetent person had been put, of all places, into the onerous as well as responsible office of schoolmaster; and his answer was significant, as well as graphic. It was, 'Wheea, he could dee nowght else. He had muddled away his land, and we put him in scheealmaster that he mou't get a bite o' brëad.' A sort of Free School it was, with a small endowment furnishing the fees for about twenty children 'put in free'. The rest of the scholars paid weekly fees at the rate of threepence for reading only, fourpence for reading and writing, and sixpence for all 'the three R's' combined. Some two

years and a half after the date of this smoke in the church, the rector of a
parish some seven miles distant from Danby, a friend of longer standing than my residence in the parish, with another beneficed clergyman
from the same neighbourhood – now the Archdeacon – came over to
call upon me, and to see how the house, which was then in process of
building with a view to its becoming the Parsonage house, was getting
on. The rising buildings duly inspected, the rector said he would like,
as we returned to my temporary dwelling, to call upon the aforesaid
minister of the parish; and to this his companion added that he would
like to pay the Free School a visit of inspection. I dissuaded him from
this project as forcibly as I could, knowing but too well what must of
necessity await him there. However, he still continued bent upon the
visit, alleging that, as he was Diocesan Inspector, it was after all no
more than his duty. Of course there was nothing that could, with
propriety, be urged against this view, and I was silent. Well, we arrived
at the school-house, a low thatched building of some antiquity, the door
of the schoolroom being reached at the end of a narrow, long, dark,
roughly paved passage. Here the noise, which had been plainly
audible outside, became very pronounced; but somehow seemed to
harmonize better with the idea of a jolly good game of romps than of
severe study. I knocked at the school door. I might as well have knocked
at the door of a smithy with half a dozen blacksmiths plying their
vocation in full swing. I knocked again, taking advantage of a partial
lull within; and this time I was heard. Silence ensued. At least, a sort of
comparative silence; for the shuffling of feet and the scraping of wooden
soles, strongly tipped with iron, upon the stone floor could be heard
only too plainly. I knocked a third time; but there was still no response,
nor any that answered, 'Come in'. So I opened the door, and motioned
the 'Inspector' to enter. The school was still enough now; for most of
the boys and girls were in their places. Only three or four small figures
could still be seen struggling under the desks, or into the places that
should have been occupied by them. But meanwhile, where was the
master? Fast asleep, and again with his tall hat on, in a large high
wooden-backed chair by the fireside. But the unwonted stillness did for
him what all the preceding hullabaloo had failed to do: – it woke him.
Rubbing his eyes with a half-comprehending consciousness, he presently recognized the presence of strangers in his abode of the Muses. His
first action was to pull off his hat; unfortunately, however, leaving a
black skull-cap on, which he was wearing under his hat. To remove

this also was his next attempt, while he staggered up to make a show of receiving his visitors. By this time the 'Inspector' had found an opportunity to whisper to me, 'Let us get away as soon as we can'; and thus terminated the first 'inspection' of the schools of this parish of Danby.

But I found myself wandering far away from the special matter I was describing, namely, my 'prospecting' visit to the parish of which I have so long been the incumbent. After my interview with the 'minister', and my visit to the church, with all the concomitant circumstances, I was at no loss to comprehend the derogatory description, given in the patron's letter, of the state of the parish as regarded from a 'church work' point of view. I could understand the slovenly, perfunctory service once a Sunday, sometimes relieved by none at all, and the consequent sleepy state of church feeling and church worship.[1] I could well understand how the only religious life in the district should be among and due to the exertions of the Wesleyans and Primitive Methodists. I could easily understand too, how the spirit of a good, right-thinking earnest-minded man like the patron of the living, one largely interested, moreover, in the welldoing and wellbeing of the many tenants who held under him, as well as more generally of the parishioners at large, would be, or rather had been, affected by finding what he, in common with so many others set in high places as to position, intelligence, and earnest zeal for the true elevation of the people, held to be one of the chief energies of improvement, so sadly in abeyance. And I hope I thought that, while I felt no great dread of the seclusion, any more than of the work I needed no one to tell me would lie before me in such a field, things might be so ordered that I might be enabled, at least in part, to become a fellow-helper in the good work which I knew right well this good and noble man wished to organize and see carried out.

I was once paying a visit to one of my elderly parishioners who was not exactly 'bed-fast', for she could get up from time to time, but being far past 'doing her own tonns' (turns), or little odds and ends of household work, was still house-fast, or unable to leave the house, even for the sake of a gossip at the next door. I found her, with her husband – a man who died a couple of years since at the age of ninety-seven – just sitting

---

[1] One of the freeholders, a steady churchman, told me not long afterwards, that within a given period – a little more than a year, as I remember his information – he had himself been to church four times oftener than the minister himself. The latter, besides being a man uninterfered with by any superfluity of energy, either bodily or intellectual, was an old and infirm man, and did not care to face the elements in bad or stormy weather.

down to tea. As a rule, I carefully avoided meal-times in all my visiting from house to house; but on the occasion I refer to there was some deviation from the customary hour for the meal just mentioned, and the old couple were going to tea at the timely hour of about half-past two in the afternoon. On finding them so engaged, I was going to retire and call in again later, or perhaps some other day. However, this did not suit the old lady's views at all, and I had to sit down and wait until their tea was satisfactorily disposed of. Naturally we fell into talk, and as the old woman had lived in the district all her life, and most of it in the near vicinity, I began to ask her questions about local matters. Within a quarter of a mile from the house we were sitting in — one of a group of three or four — was a place commonly known by the name 'Fairy Cross Plains'. I asked her, Could she tell me why the said place was so called? 'Oh yes,' she replied: 'just a little in front of where the public-house at the Plains now stood, in the old days before the roads were made as they were now, two ways or roads used to cross, and that gave the "cross" part of the name. And as to the rest of it, or the name "Fairy", everybody knew that years and years ago the fairies had "a desper't haunt o' thae hill-ends just ahint the Public".' I certainly had heard as much over and over again, and so could not profess myself to be such a nobody as to be ignorant of the circumstance. Among others, a man with whom I was brought into perpetual contact, from the relative positions we occupied in the parish — he was, and is, parish clerk — had told me that his childhood had been spent in the immediate vicinity of 'the Plains', and that the fairy-rings just above the inn in question were the largest and the most regular and distinct he had ever seen any-where. He and the other children of the hamlet used constantly to amuse themselves by running round and round in these rings; but they had always been religiously careful never to run quite nine times round any one of them. 'Why not?' I asked. 'Why, sir, you see that if we had run the full number of nine times, that would have given the fairies power over us, and they would have come and taken us away for good, to go and live where they lived.' — 'But,' said I, 'you do not believe that, surely, Peter?' — 'Why, yes, we did then, sir,' he answered, 'for the mothers used to threaten us, if we wer'n't good, that they would turn us to the door (out of doors) at night, and then the fairies would get us.'

But to return to the old woman with whom I was conversing. I admitted that I had both heard of and seen the fairy-rings in question;

but what about the fairies themselves? Had anybody ever seen them? 'Ay, many a tahm and offens,' said she; 'they used to come down the hill by this deear (door), and gaed in at yon brig-steean,' indicating a large culvert which conveyed the water of a small beck underneath the road about a stone's throw from the cottage. A further question elicited the reply that it was a little green man, with a queer sort of a cap on him, that had been seen in the act of disappearing in this culvert. Just here the old woman's husband broke in with the query, 'Wheea, where do they live, then?' – 'Why, under t' grund, to be seear (sure).' 'Neea, neea,' says the old man, 'how can they live under t' grund?' The prompt rejoinder was, 'Why, t' moudiwarps (moles) dis, an' wheea not not t' fairies?' This shut him up, and he collapsed forthwith. His wife, however, was now in the full flow of communicativeness, and to my question, Had she ever herself seen a fairy? the unhesitating reply was, 'Neea, but Ah've heared 'em offens.' I thought I was on the verge of a tradition similar to that of the Claymore Well, at no great distance from Kettleness, where, as 'everybody used to ken.' the fairies in days of yore were wont to wash their clothes and to bleach and beat them, and on their washing nights the strokes of the 'battledoor' – that is, the old-fashioned implement for smoothing newly-washed linen, which has been superseded by the mangle – were heard as far as Runswick. But it was not so. What my interlocutor had heard were the sounds indicative of the act of butter-making; sounds familiar enough to those acquainted with the old forms of making up the butter in a good-sized Dales dairy. These sounds, she said, she had very often heard when she lived servant at such and such a farm. Moreover, although she had never set eyes on the butter-makers themselves, she had frequently seen the produce of their labour, that is to say, the 'fairy-butter'; and she proceeded to give me the most precise details as to its appearance, and the place where she found it. There was a certain gate, on which she had good reason to be sure, on one occasion, there was none overnight; but she had heard the fairies at their work 'as plain as plain, and in the morning the butter was clamed (smeared) all over main part o' t' gate.'

But her fairy reminiscences were by no means exhausted, even by such a revelation as this. She had known a lass quite well, who one day, when raking in the hayfield, had raked over a fairy bairn. 'It was liggin' in a swathe of the half-made hay, as bonny a lahtle thing as ever yan seen. But it was a fairy-bairn, it was quite good to tell. But it did not stay lang wi' t' lass at fun' (found) it. It a soort o' dwinied away, and she aimed (supposed) the fairy-mother couldn't deea wivout it any langer.' Here again I was a little disappointed. I had expected to get hold of a genuine unsophisticated changeling story, localized and home-bred. But the termination was as I have just recorded.

From fairies the old lady got on to recollections of what clearly was a survival of dwarf folklore. For she told me of certain small people who used to dwell in the houes (gravemounds) that years ago were to be found in the Roxby and Mickleby direction, but which had been dug into and afterwards ploughed over, so that the former denizens had clearly been evicted and forced to retire. But it was only imperfect recollections of what she had heard in her own young days that my informant was dealing with now; and the lack of feature and detail consequent on her lack of personal interest in the subject was quite evident. But it was quite different when I began to ask her if in her youth she had had any knowledge of the Hart Hall 'Hob'. On this topic she was herself again. 'Why, when she was a bit of a lass, everybody knew about Hart Hall in Glaisdale, and t' Hob there, and the work that he did, and how he came to leave, and all about it.' Had she ever seen him, or any of the work he had done? 'Seen him, saidst 'ee? Neea, naebody had ever seen him, leastwise, mair nor yance. And that was how he coomed to flit.' – 'How was that?' I asked. 'Wheea, everybody kenned at sikan a mak' o' creatur as yon never tholed being spied efter.' – 'And did they spy upon him?' I inquired. 'Ay, marry, that did they. Yah moonleeght neeght, when they heared his swipple (the striking part of the flail) gannan' wiv a strange quick bat (stroke) o' t' lathe fleear (on the barn floor) – ye ken he wad dee mair i' yah neeght than a' t' men o' t' farm cou'd dee iv a deea – yan i' t' lads gat hissel' croppen oop close anenst lathe-deear, an' leeake'd in thruff a lahtle hole i' t' boards, an' he seen a lahtle brown man, a' covered wi' hair, spangin' about wiv fleeal alhk yan wud (striking around with the flail as if he was beside himself). He'd getten a haill dess o' shaffs (a whole layer of sheaves) doon o' t' fleear, and my wo'd! ommost afore ye cou'd tell ten, he had tonned (turned) oot t' strae, an' sided away t' coorn, and was rife for another dess. He had nae claes on to speak of, and t' lad, he cou'd na see at he had any mak' or mander o' duds by an au'd ragg'd soort ov a sark.' And she went on to tell how the lad crept away as quietly as he had gone on his expedition of espial, and on getting indoors, undiscovered by the unconscious Hob, had related what he had seen, and described the marvellous energy of 't' lahtle hairy man, amaist as nakt as when he wur boorn.' But the winter nights were cold, and the Hart Hall folks thought he must get strange and warm working 'sikan a bat as yon, an' it wad be sair an' cau'd for him, gannan' oot iv lathe wiv nobbut thae au'd rags. Seear, they'd mak' him something to hap hissel' wiv.' And so they did. They made it as near like what the boy had described him as wearing – a sort of a coarse sark, or shirt, with a belt or girdle to confine it round his middle. And when it was done, it was taken before nightfall and laid in the barn, 'gay and handy for t' lahtle chap to notish' when next he came to resume his nocturnal labours. In due course he came, espied the garment, turned it round and round, and – contrary to the usual termination of such legends, which represents the uncanny, albeit efficient, worker as displeased at the espionage practised upon him – Hart Hall Hob, more mercenary than punctilious as to considerations of privacy, broke out with the following couplet—

> *Gin Hob mun hae nowght but a hardin' hamp,*
> *He'll coom nae mair, nowther to berry nor stamp.*

I pause a moment in my narrative here to remark that this old jingle or rhyme is one of no ordinary or trifling interest. It seems almost superfluous to suggest that up to half a century ago, and even later, there was hardly a place in all Her Majesty's English dominions better qualified to be conservative of the old words of the ordinary folk-speech, as well as of the old notions, legends, usages, beliefs, such as constitute its folklore, than this particular part of the district of Cleveland. The simple fact that its Glossary comprises near upon four thousand words, and that still the supply is not fully exhausted, speaks volumes on that head. And yet this couplet preserves three words, all of which had become obsolete forty years ago, and two of which had no actual meaning to the old dame who repeated the rhyme to me. These two are 'berry' and 'hamp'. 'Stamp' was the verb used to express the action of knocking off the awns of the barley previously to threshing it, according to the old practice. But 'berry', meaning to thresh, I had been looking and inquiring for, for years, and looking and inquiring in vain; and as to 'hamp', I never had reason to suppose that it had once been a constituent part of the current Cleveland folkspeech. But this is not all. The meaning of the word, and no less the description given of the vestment in question, in the legend itself, throws back the origin, at least the form-taking, of the story, and its accompaniments, to an indefinite, and yet dimly definable period. There was a time when the hamp was the English peasant's only garment; at all events, mainly or generally so. For it might sometimes be worn over some underclothing. But that was not the rule. The hamp was a smockfrock-like article of raiment gathered in somewhat about the middle, and coming some little way below the knee. The mention in *Piers the Plowman* of the 'hatere' worn by the labouring man in his day serves to give a fairly vivid idea of the attire of the working-man of that time, and that attire was the 'hamp' of our northern parts. For the word seems to be clearly Old Danish in form and origin. But although the form and fashion and accessories of our old lady's stories were of so distinctly an old-world character, it was impossible to doubt for a moment her perfect good faith. She told all with the most utter simplicity, and the most evident conviction that what she was telling was matter of faith, and not at all the flimsy structure of fancy or of fable.

Neither the fairies of Fairy Cross Plains nor the Glaisdale Hob were unrealities to her mind. They might not be now; but they had been, as certainly as her own remote fore-elders, and much more certainly than Oliver Cromwell or Julius Caesar. And I have noticed the same sort of underlying implicit faith in more than one or two of my hard-headed, shrewd matter-of-fact Yorkshire neighbours, dwellers in these deep, retired, and, fifty years ago, almost out-of-the-world dales of ours, when once I had succeeded in breaking through the outside husk of semi-suspicion and reserve instinctively worn as a shield by the mind of the unlearned when newly roused by the prickings of doubt or the questionings of incredulity. I have often found it very difficult to get them to speak with any approach to unreserve on the topics which lie nearest to the very core of our most interesting folklore. One old man in particular, as simple-minded, honest, truth-loving, and, I always believed, as good and God-fearing a man as I ever met with, who had a great personal regard for me, and besides was drawn to me by my connection with the place of his birth and the people of his father's house, as well as by the official intercourse which his position as master of the Union House at Guisborough, and mine as guardian of the poor for the parish, had involved during a period of several years, was, with the greatest difficulty, led on to speak at all, and much more to talk freely, about such matters. I knew from many sources and circumstances that he was a veritable storehouse and magazine of folklore subjects and ex-

periences – I use the latter word advisedly – and recollections. In the
course of our business relations there was too much on his hands and
on mine to admit of our 'hoddin' pross' (holding a gossiping talk)
about such matters as 'wafts' (Scottice, wraiths), or 'wise men'
(Anglice, wizards, soothsayers, or conjurers);[1] but some little while
after he had ceased to wear the official dignity just named, having been
pensioned off in consideration of long and faithful service, I rode over
to his abode, partly to pay my old friend a visit, and partly to try if I
could in any way induce him to talk to me freely about the matters
which were of interest to me as a folklore inquirer, and which I knew
had greatly occupied, and perhaps exercised, his mind through years of
his long life. It was long before I could get him to enter upon the subject at all. His scruples were partly of a religious nature – there was so
much that seemed uncanny in his recollections, so much that his unsophisticated mind could not but refer, directly or indirectly, to the
agency of something unhallowed, if not to 't' au'd Donnot' himself –
but partly they were due to the fear of being thought credulous or
superstitious; and partly, no doubt, to a suspicion that many or most
among his questioners and interlocutors on such topics would most
likely be trying to draw him out on purpose to make fun of his old-
world tales, and treat him as an object of ridicule and mockery. His
anterior knowledge of me, and personal respect and regard for me,

[1] This is a word which had some few years ago, if it has not still, its full and true sense in
this part of the world. Some forty years ago, when country-parsons, or, as we were called
throughout this district, 'Church-priests,' were not so distinguished by their cleric attire,
or clerical pursuits, or clerical activity, either Sunday or 'war-day,' as they have come to
be since, and when I was seldom walking less than thirty-five or forty miles weekly in my
church and house-to-house work, an elderly woman living about half a mile from my
house, and who had been used otherwise than well in her younger days, and in consequence was not quite sound as to some particulars in her intellect, sent to me urgently one
day to go to her house, for she was in much trouble. I had seen her often, both at my
residence and her own, and had a shrewd suspicion as to the nature of her trouble, and
that it was spiritual, in a sense, although perhaps not quite within the province of the
parish priest. On going to her house I found poor old Dinah was much troubled indeed.
She told me the house was fairly taken possession of by spirits, and that, turn which way
she would, she was beset by them. She told me what spirits they were, and in some
instances whose spirits, and what their objects and efforts were, and she had sent for me
that I should 'lay them'. I tried to soothe her, and talked to her in the endeavour to divert
her thoughts into a more reasonable channel. She was perfectly clear and reasonable on
every other topic; but do what I would, and represent what I could, her mind continually
reverted to the one subject that possessed her, namely, the actual presence of the spirits.
I told her at last I could not, did not profess to 'lay spirits'; and her reply was, 'Ay, but if
I had sent for a priest o' t' au'd church, he wad a' deean it. They wur a vast mair powerful
conjurers than you Church-priests.'

combined with my already well-known and unquestionably sincere interest in what I wanted him to tell me about, prevailed at last, and he began to discourse freely. He soon warmed to his subject, and there came a flow of reminiscences, personal experiences and impressions, reflections, considerations, and remarks, that kept him occupied as the chief speaker for well on to a couple of hours. And all through, from beginning to end, there was not a word or a look or a gesture to even suggest a doubt or a question, I must not say as to the entire truthfulness of his narratives, for that was transparent, but of his own implicit but unconscious conviction that he was relating to me the plain unvarnished tale of what had actually taken place under his own observation, or within the scope of his own personal knowledge. He told me much that he could not explain, much that was quite beyond his comprehension, much that he clearly looked upon as very questionable in its origin or inspiration, but which he had seen or heard, and no more thought of questioning than his own being, present and future, because no doubt either of one or the other had ever suggested itself to his simple mind.

Another case of the same sort was that of one of the worthiest of my many worthy parishioners, a man sensible, clear-headed, intelligent, one of my best helpers in all good and useful things as long as he was spared for this life's works, a man with the instinctive feelings of the truest gentility, but who always seemed averse to entering on any folklore talk or inquiry, and was, even admittedly, on his guard lest he should be led on to speak of them inadvertently. Twice, and twice only, I got him into conference with me on the, by him, tabooed subject-matters; and on both occasions it was equally a surprise both to him and to me. In either case an accidental remark was like a spark by chance firing a train ready laid, but not laid for the special purpose of firing that special mine. And on both occasions not only did I succeed in collecting some of the very most interesting details it has ever become my good fortune to meet with, but I saw that my usually recalcitrant informer was strangely impressed with what he was telling me in connection in which I had put it.[1] One of these subjects was the careful ceremonial to be observed in the obtaining of effectual 'witch-wood' for the incoming year; and the other, one that led on to the dis-

[1] This was my friend William Robinson of Fryup Head. What he told me about the care necessary in obtaining effectual witch-wood is recorded at p. 48. John Unthank's communications touching the Wise Man will be found pp. 55 et seq..

covery of an original act of Odin-worship in one of the commonest, most every-day practices of all the farmers and occupiers of the district, as they were five-and-twenty or thirty years ago, not a few of them doing the same thing to this day.

But perhaps the most striking illustration that can be given of the tacit, unsuspected, but still implicit faith, in the Dales folks' minds, in old folklore usages and customs is as follows. This used to be, and still is to a considerable extent, largely a dairy district. The farms are none of them large, there not being half a dozen in the parish much over a hundred acres in extent. Nevertheless, dairies of ten or twelve cows each used to be the rule on these larger farms. And it is alleged as a fact, and by no means without reason or as contrary to experience, that if one of the cows in a dairy unfortunately produces a calf prematurely – in local phrase, 'picks her cau'f' – the remainder of the cows in the same building are only too likely, or too liable, to follow suit; of course to the serious loss of the owner. The old-world prophylactic or folklore-prescribed preventative in such a contingency used to be to remove the threshold of the cow-house in which the mischance had befallen, dig a deep hole in the place so laid bare, deep enough, indeed, to admit of the abortive calf being buried in it, on its back, with its four legs all stretching vertically upwards in the rigidity of death, and then to cover all up as before.

Now, I had good reason for feeling assured that this had been actually done on a farmstead no very great way distant from my dwelling, and almost within the term of my own personal acquaintance with the place; as also I had reason to believe that it had been done more than once, within the same limit of time, in more than one of the adjacent dales to the south of us. Wishing to be fully assured of the first-named circumstance as a fact, I took the opportunity afforded by a casual meeting with the occupant of the farm just referred to – in point of fact a son of the alleged performer of the said rite or observance, and a regular hard-headed, shrewd, independent-willed Yorkshireman, now dead, poor fellow – to ask him if he knew of the continued existence of the said usage, adding that I had heard of it as still practised in Farndale. 'Ay,' he said, 'there's many as dis it yet. My au'd father did it. But it's sae mony years syne, it must be about wore out by now, and I shall have to dee it again.' Poor George Nicholson's faith needed no greater confirmation as a still living faith than this. But the like characteristics were not merely present they were probably evident in the case of each of the other persons I have mentioned. The old woman in Fryup, the ex-Union House master, my much regretted old friend, all spoke of the matters they talked to me about as things that had been, and were real, and not as creations of the fancy, or old-wives' tales and babble.

CHAPTER TWO

Hob at Work

BUT we left our old lady in the midst of her 'Hob' reminiscences, which, as I have said, and emphasized in the last chapter, she told with a sort of personal recollection of them, rather than as what had been told her by others, or handed down from one teller of the old, old story to another. One of her tellings was that the people of the farm in question, or Hart Hall in Glaisdale, had been leading – that is, carting – hay in a 'catchy' time, when every load got was a load saved, as if by snatching from the wilfulness of the weather; and another load had been won, and was creeping its slow way towards the 'staggarth', when, as ill-luck would have it, one of the wheels of the wain slipped in between two of the 'coverers of a brigstone',[1] and there remained fast and inextricable by any easily applicable force. Extra horse-power was fetched; men applied their shoulders to the wheel; gave-locks were brought and efforts made to lever the wheel out of its fix; but all equally in vain; and there seemed nothing for it – awkward as such a place was for the purpose, for the brigstone lay across a gate-stead – but to 'teem' (empty) the hay out of the vehicle, and liberate it when thus lightened of its load. But it was too late in the day to do that at once, with prudence, even had the weather been much less uncertain that it was. And so, with whatever unwillingness, the load was left for the night under its detainer, and all hands were to be set to work the first thing in the morning to effect its liberation. But there was one about the place who

[1] A brigstone is a kind of rough conduit for water across a gate-stead, or even a road of greater pretension, made by paving the bottom of a transverse trench or channel, dug on purpose, with flagstones, setting up other flags on either side as walls, and covering all in with other slabs of stone of sufficient solidity to upbear any loaded vehicle likely to be driven across the said conduit. The 'coverers' are the slabs just mentioned, laid over all; and, from wear and tear, or natural decay, it not infrequently happens that the interspace between two coverers widens by degrees, however closely the edges may have been laid at first, until, on some unlucky occasion, a wheel a little narrower than usual, or grinding along under a load heavy enough to break a bit from the attenuated edge, forces its way down and betwixt, and remains a fixture, even if it does not occasion an overthrow.

thought scorn of waiting for the morrow for such a trifling business as that, and when the wearied and worried household had retired to bed, Hob went forth in his mysterious might, made no difficulty about extricating the locked-in wheel, and trailing the cumbersome load up the steep, broken road to the homestead, putting the hay in beautiful order on the stack, and setting the wain ready for the leading that would of course be renewed early in the morning.

This was but one of the many exploits of a like nature achieved by this well-willed being in aid of the work on that favoured farm. In the barn, if there was a 'weight of work' craving to be done, and time was scant or force insufficient, Hob would come unasked, unwarned, to the rescue, and the corn would be threshed, dressed, and sacked, nobody knew how, except that it was done by the Hob. Unaccountable strength seemed to be the chief attribute ascribed to him. One did not hear of him as mowing or reaping, ploughing, sowing, or harrowing; but what mortal strength was clearly incapable of, that was the work which Hob took upon himself. Another thing to be remarked about this Hob – at least in all the stories about him and his doings – was that there was no reminiscence of his mischievousness, harmless malice, or even trickiness. He was not of those who resent, with a sort of pettish, or even spiteful, malice, the possibly unintended interference with elfish prerogative implied in stopping up an 'awfbore' or hole in deal-boarding occasioned by the dropping out of a shrunken knot, and which displayed itself in the way of forcibly ejecting the intended stopping, in the form of a sharply driven pellet, into the face, or directly on to the nose, of the offender. Neither was he like the Farndale Hob told of by Professor Phillips (among other chroniclers), who was so 'familiar and troublesome a visitor of one of the farmers of the dale, and caused him so much vexation and petty loss, that he resolved to quit his house in Farndale and seek some other home. Early in the morning, as he was on his way, with his household goods in a cart, a neighbour meeting him said, "Ah sees thou's flitting." – "Ay," cries Hob out of the churn, "ay, we'se flittin'." On which the farmer, concluding that change of abode would not rid him of his troublesome inmate, turned his horse's head homeward again.'

I am sorry it has never fallen to my lot to hear this last story from one of the people – one of the 'folk' themselves. In that case, I am certain it would have assumed a very different aspect. I have not given an exact copy of Professor Phillips's version, and for this reason – that the whole story is in reality a mere travesty. The story never was, and never could be, told in that form, and with such 'properties' as are given by the author in question. He speaks of the neighbour who meets the flitting farmer as 'addressing him in good Yorkshire'. It would be a strange thing indeed if a Farndale farmer even now spoke anything else except 'good Yorkshire'. He makes him carry all his 'household goods and gods' on one cart. He causes him to suspend and reverse all his flitting proceedings, quite regardless of what a flitting is, and how subject to a set of sufficiently fixed and stated rules, as to period or term, succession of one tenant to another, and so forth. He seems to me entirely unaware that a 'flitting' is, like matrimony, 'not to be lightly or wantonly taken in hand'; and, still less, abandoned after the said fashion. And besides, he makes a 'play on the vowel' in the words, 'Ay, we are flutting', which he puts into the mouth of the Hob, and which is simply nonsensical when all is taken into account. Such a play on the vowel is alien to the district; and a Farndale man would be fully as likely to say 'hutting' for 'hitting', 'sutting' for 'sitting', or 'mutten' for 'mitten', as 'flutting' for 'flitting'. Reference is also made to the Scandinavian version of the story. But that, as told by Worsaae himself, is reasonable and to the point; and is true as to the characteristics in which Phillips goes astray. Certainly the Danish professor calls the being of whom the story is told 'Nisse', instead of 'Hob', as he calls the human actor in the drama by his Danish epithet 'bonde' instead of English 'farmer'; but he steers clear of the mistake of calling the Nisse 'a daemon', which is the term applied by the English professor to poor soulless Hob. 'In England,' says Worsaae, 'one may hear many a tale told, just as in Danish lands, about the tricksiness of the Nisse (Nix). On one occasion during my stay in England, it occurred to me to tell our northern story about a "bonde" (a word nearly equivalent to our English "yeoman") who was teased and annoyed in all sorts of ways by a Nisse. At last, he could not stand it any longer, and he determined to quit his holding, and to go to some other spot. When he had conveyed nearly all his movables to his new farm, and was just driving the last load of all, he happened to turn round, and what was the sight that met his eyes? Nothing less than Master Nisse himself, red cap and all, calmly perched on the top of the load. The small chap nodded with provoking familiarity, and added the words, "Ay, here we are, flitting".' But there is no play on the vowel in Worsaae's Danish. It is just the ordinary Danish phrase, 'Nu flytte vi,' which is employed.

Worsaae adds that the English counterpart – almost word for word (*naesten ord till andet*) – was found by him localized in Lancashire; and it is possible Phillips's version is not really of Yorkshire origin at all, although localized by him in Farndale. For I do not doubt that, misconceived and mistakenly coloured as the features of the story as told by him are, the change of the vowel may have a significance. Times without number I have heard the word 'bushel' sounded 'bishel'; the personal name 'Ridsdale' is commonly 'Rudsdale' in Cleveland at the present day; and I have many instances in which the bishopric (of Durham, namely) is written 'busshoprick' in the first James's time and later, and written so, moreover, in the official Records kept by the Clerk of the Peace of the time. It is possible, therefore, that, if the story as given by Professor Phillips is not in reality derived from a Lancashire, a County of Durham, or a Scottish Border source, the presence of the form 'flutting' in it may be of antiquarian significance, and betoken that such form of the tale indicates an antiquity of not less than from two to three centuries, and quite possibly even much more than that: that, in other words, the terms 'hamp', 'berry', and 'stamp' of the couplet given above, and the 'flutting' of this Hob story, are correlative as to the inference we are, in either case, more than simply enabled to make as to the hoary antiquity of the Hob legends.

And yet our communicative old lady told forth her tale as of things that had happened under everybody's cognizance, and as it might be only the other day; and of which she had only just missed personal cognizance herself by coming a little too late on the scene. She told her story of the doings and disappearance of Hob, and of the fairy dancing, of their retreat to their underground habitations, and 'bittling' their clothes, of the finding of the fairy-bairn, in precisely the same tone and manner as I was told in after years by divers of the folks in the same vicinity, who only had not been actual eye-witnesses, of the marvellous escape of a child sleeping between two adults in their bed in a cottage no great way distant, and yet coming forth scatheless, although both his companions had been struck dead in a moment by lightning; and she told her story of the butter-making as of a thing the actuality of which was so assured that it never entered her imagination to suppose it could be questioned.

Of course such an unpremeditated, unintended assumption of personal experience, such a spontaneous disclosure of personal conviction, made the telling very effective; and if it could be appropriated and employed

at will by the *viva voce* story-teller, would forthwith make his fortune.
But that is a point by the way, which need not be dwelt upon. The thing
really worth notice is the deep hold these divers matters of overtrow
had gotten, and had continued to hold, not only on the imagination,
but on the uncultured mind of our dale-dwellers of even less than a
century ago. But if, in saying this, or in anything that I have previously
advanced, I have led on to the idea that I hold these people to be, in any
true practical sense of the word, a 'superstitious' people, I shall have
conveyed a wrong impression. I have met with any number of educated,
cultured people who devoutly believe that suffering the sun to shine
freely upon a fire in the ordinary grate puts it out; that setting a poker
vertically up against the fire grate in front of it, causes the smouldering,
nearly extinct fire to burn brightly up; that the changes of the moon
influence the changes of the weather; that even the coincidence of
certain phases of the moon with certain days of the week exercises a
disastrous influence upon the weather of the ensuing days of the week,
or month; that a great profusion of hedge-fruit – 'hips and haws'
especially – betokens, not a past favourable fruiting season, but the
severity of the coming winter; and so forth. Now all this is what I
would willingly call 'overtrow', or believing overmuch, not 'superstition': which word, as Professor Skeat tells us, is due to the elder
French *superstition*, which is derived from *superstitionem*, the accusative
of Latin *superstitio*, and means 'a standing still over or near a thing,
amazement, wonder, dread, religious scruple'. Now there was no more
dread, nor even wonder or amazement, in the simple minds of these
worthy parishioners of mine, than there is in the mind of the refined
and cultured lady who leans the poker against the top bar of her draw-
ing-room grate to draw the fire up, or puts down the venetian blind to
prevent the sun extinguishing the fire that seemd to be dulled by the
superior brightness of his rays. The nearest approach to the feeling – I
must not say of dread, or even apprehension, so much as – of precaution that I have ever met with was in the case of a farm-lass in
Farndale, who, hearing the 'gabble-ratchet'[1] overhead, as she was
coming in from the fold-yard to the house in the dusk of the evening,
rushed hastily indoors, slammed to door to, bolted it, and flung her
apron over her head. On being asked, 'What was the matter?' her

---

[1] A name for a yelping sound at night, like the cry of hounds, and probably due to
flocks of wild geese flying by night. Taken as an omen of approaching death. See my
Glossary of Cleveland Dialect, sub voce.

answer was, 'I heared t' gabble-ratcher; but I lay I've stopped it fra deeing me any ho't (hurt).' Or I might quote another and entirely analogous instance. In the days when there was no lime procurable here otherwise than by sending waggons with their full teams over the moor to Hutton le Hole, or some such place, the journey was often one which, beginning at four o clock in the morning, was not concluded until eight at night. It was at the close of just one of these tedious, wearisome expeditions that the farm-servant on one of the farms in Fryup Head was loosing out his weary 'draught' (team), and the willing farm-lass was lending a helping hand, when they saw in the swampy, undrained 'swang' lying some quarter or third of a mile below the house on the border of the beck, a will-o'-the-wisp, or in local nomen-clature, a 'Jenny-wi'-t'-lant'ren.' The man turned his jacket inside out and the girl turned her apron; after which they proceeded placidly with their occupation, troubling themselves no more about the misleading propensities and powers of the assumed personal entity just named.

Not that I suppose there was any real or deep-seated dread or apprehension, or any feeling allied to either, which led to the adoption of these precautionary measures in these last two instances. I don't believe for a moment that the Fryup Head man and lass supposed the Jack o' Lanthorn would actually come up from the swamp and try to bewilder and mislead them where they were; nor that the Farndale maiden believed that the omen would have a personal application to herself had she omitted the ceremonies named in her case. The feeling in action in either case may be difficult to analyse, but I do not think it is hard to comprehend. I was walking one day, many years ago, with a very old and a very dear friend of mine, only just out of this immediate neighbourhood, when a magpie flew across the line of our path. My friend, a solicitor in a large practice, and holding the position of Deputy Clerk of the Peace, as well as that of Clerk to the local Bench of Magi-strates, a wise and a good man, with such opportunities of insight into the workings of human nature as such a position forced upon him, took off his hat with the greatest ceremony, and so saluted the bird in its passage. On my remarking on the circumstance, 'Oh,' said he, 'I always take off my hat to a magpie.' And I myself was always in the habit of turning all the money I had in my pocket on the first sight of the new moon, until one day another old friend of mine completely disillusioned me by remarking, when he saw me busy in the accustomed way, 'Why, what's the use of doing that? You always see the moon through glass,' in allusion to my invariably-worn spectacles. And it is but a week since I saw a lady stoop down in one of the most frequented streets in York, deliberately pick up a horse-shoe which lay by the side of the flags of the foot-pavement, as deliberately deposit it in the natty lady's light basket she was carrying, and I was quite well aware that it would be heedfully borne off home, and hung, as I knew nearly a dozen predecessors were already hung; but fruitlessly and in vain, as I had often told her, because they were hung as they could be hung on a nail – and that is, with the toe upwards; and not, as everybody ought to know, with their hinder ends or heel upwards – a matter which, unless it be attended to, completely invalidates the efficiency of the prophylactic power of the accidentally found but observantly picked up horse-shoe.

And yet it was not 'superstition', in either of its graduated senses as tabulated by Professor Skeat, which induced any of the three actors above mentioned to do as they did. It was not even 'overtrow'. For no one of the three for one moment believed or imagined, entertained so much as the initial germ of a conception, that we should be advantaged in reality, even by the mass of a mote in the sunbeam, by what we did; or, on the other hand, disadvantaged by its omission. There was a sort of 'use and wont' in it, which, though in a certain sense 'honoured in its observance', it was felt in some sort of indirect, unmeditated, unvolitional sort of way, would not be dishonoured in the breach.

And something of the same sort, as I take it, was the condition or attitude of mind in these old friends of mine who, divers of them, and on divers and manifold occasions, have told me such stories and traditions as the above with so much *empressement* and apparently evident conviction of the reality of what they were relating. I do not say that I think it was so always; that there had never been a time when there was absolutely a faith of a sort in that which furnished the basis of all these narratives, a superstition really, and not a mere harmless exhibition of overtrow. Thus, for instance, I have no doubt at all of the very real and the very deep-seated existence of a belief in the actuality and the power of the witch. Nay, I make no doubt whatever that the witch herself, in multitudes of instances, believed in her own power quite as firmly as any of those who had learned to look upon her with a dread almost reminding one of the African dread of fetish. Fifty years ago the whole atmosphere of the folklore firmament in this district was so surcharged with the being and the works of the witch, that one seemed able to trace her presence and her activity in almost every nook and corner of the neighbourhood. But this is far too wide and deep and intricate a subject to be entered upon at the close of a section already quite sufficiently long.

It is not yet twenty-five years since a member of the Society of Friends, himself a very shrewd and observant man, as well as a successful tradesman in a considerable market-town in Cleveland, when talking to me about some of the different matters which he knew were of interest to me, touched not only on the general subject of folklore, but on the specific branch of it furnished by witchcraft, and the extensive and, in some part, still current belief in it; and he gave me the following anecdote in illustration of what he was advancing. 'Not long since,' he began, 'a woman very well known to me as a neighbour and more than a merely occasional customer, came into my shop, and after making her purchases, took out her purse for the purpose of paying for the goods bought. In doing so she dropped something which had been in the pocket together with the purse. A close and very diligent search for the object that had fallen ensued immediately. But it was apparently in vain, and it continued to be in vain for so long that I asked her what she had lost. For a space she seemed shy of telling me; but at last she replied, "I have lost my witch-wood; and it will never do to be without that." — "Why, Mally," I said in reply, "surely you don't believe in witches?" "Not believe in witches, saidst 'ee? Wheea, Ah kens weel there's eleven in G— at this present tahm (time)! Neea, neea, it will na dee to be wivout my witch-wood!"' But not only was there this still current and widely-spread faith in the witch, in her influence as well as her malevolence, but not a few of the stories current were such as to imply absolute conviction on the part of the witch herself of the actual possession of the powers she was credited with. I do not mean that under terror of possible application of some modified sort of 'question' or torture, or the pressure of actual cruelty, they admitted the imputation of witchcraft, nor even that for sinister purposes they laid claim to the possession of the powers implied; but that, whether under the influence of an excited credulity, or possibly a condition allied to if not identical with that spoken of as 'magnetic', 'hypnotic', or 'mesmeric', they might verily and really conceive themselves to be possessed of the alleged powers, and adopt both the language and the action consonant thereto. Indeed I can hardly conceive that it could possibly be otherwise.

More than forty years ago, a very noteworthy proportion of witch stories were not only localized, but the names, the personality, the actual identity of the witches of greatest repute or notoriety were precisely specified and detailed. I have had houses in three or four of the townships of this immediate district pointed out to me as the abodes of this or that 'noted witch'. In Danby, Westerdale, Glaisdale, Farndale, as well as farther afield, this place or that, and sometimes to the number of two or three in a single one of the parishes named, has been indicated as the scene of this or that strange experience springing out of witch-craft, or of some stranger exploit in the same connection. Here the witch was baffled by the employment of an agency more potent than her own (of which more at a future page), here she was irresistible or triumphant; there she came to grief, perhaps through the use of silver slugs fired at her, perhaps through some other of the accredited means for neutralizing her power or damaging her person. In one of these stories, perhaps as graphic as any I have met with, and which to my regret I am unable to give in detail by reason of the nature of the means, or at least the effect of the means, employed for the purpose of bringing the witch to book, her name and abode as well as those of her victim being given with all precision, she is brought on the scene as forced to confess her misdeeds, and constrained to remain in a condition of sheer bodily purgatory until she had removed the spell laid on her victim and his goods, and besides that remedied its baneful effects. Another, in which the self-same uncanny old lady is the principal actor, and even-tually the actual sufferer, runs thus: A party of freeholders, mainly if not exclusively belonging to Westerdale, were out coursing, but had met with no success, not having found a single hare in the course of their long morning's quest. When thinking of giving up their pursuit as hopeless, they fell in with old Nanny —, the most 'noted witch' in all the countryside. No long time passed before she was made aware by the disappointed sportsmen – and some thought she knew it all before – of their failure to find a hare, and much more of getting a course. 'Oh,' says the wrinkled, hook-nosed, crook-backed old dame, 'I can tell you where you will find a hare ligging, and a grand one and all. I'se ho'd ye (I will undertake to you) she'll gi'e ye a grand course. Only, whativver ye deea, minnd ye dinna slip a black dog at her! That wad be a sair matter for ye all.' They gave their word to attend to this injunction, and proceeded to the locality the old dame indicated. There, sure enough, they found a noble hare, which went away gallantly before the two dogs slipped at her. I ought to mention that the names and abodes of all the party were mentioned to me in detail by my informant; the place at which the interview with the witch took place, the place where she told them to seek the hare and found her, and the line of country taken by the quarry, with the places where the greyhounds 'turned' her, and all the particulars of a most exciting and, to sportsmen, interesting course. In short, the hare led them a chase of several miles over parts of the Westerdale moors, over the Ingleby boundary, circling back by Hob Hole till she had nearly reached the spot where she was originally met with. Here, as luck would have it, a black dog, not belonging to any one of the party, and coming no one knew whence, suddenly joined in the course, and just as the hitherto unapproachable hare made a final effort to get through a smout-hole at the foot of the wall of the garth in which the cot of the reputed witch was situate – and the habitation in question is a habitation still – the black dog, according to the expression used, 'threw at her', but succeeded in little more than tearing out some of the fleck of her haunch, bringing with it, in one place, a bit of the skin. That was the end of the course, but not of the story. It continued thus: The party after a pause, due, as it would seem, in part to apprehension, and, in the case of one at least, to suspicion, went to Nanny's door, and, although it was fast, succeeded eventually in obtaining admission. The apprehensive members of the party, having a wholesome fear of witch-prowess in general, and of Nanny's in particular – especially in consideration of their live stock – desired to excuse themselves for the inadvertent violation of her injunction as to the colour of the dogs which were to be permitted to join in the course. One of them, however, as just intimated, more suspicious or better informed than his comrades, wished to satisfy himself as to the presence and the condition of old Nanny herself. Finding admission to the dwelling, in the cots of the time, was finding admission to the sleeping apartment and all. For there were no chambers upstairs then. There was the living room, with a sort of boxed-off place or two for sleeping arrangements, and perhaps a roost for the fowls; but nothing beyond in the way of more modern refinements. And when the party entered, there was old Nanny stretched on her bed, disabled and in pain. 'What was wrang wiv 'er? She had been weel enough but a bit afore.' – 'Eh, she had happened an accident, and lamed hersen.' But the suspicions of the suspicious one were allowed to prevail, and the old woman's hurts were overhauled, and it was found she was rent as if by a dog's teeth on the haunch, exactly where the hare, which had run through the smout into

Nanny's garth, had been seen to be seized by the unlucky (and un-welcome) black dog.

There was another Nanny, of Danby celebrity, who lived in a house of precisely the same character as the Westerdale Nanny's, situate about half a mile to the east of the house in which this is written. I have no doubt that she was really an 'historical' character, and that the plain English of many of the stories that have been told me about her is that she was an object of persecution by the 'young bloods' of the day and district, – young fellows of the farming persuasion, the sons of free-holders, or possibly freeholders themselves. But the story I would relate came to me in much the following form. 'Au'd Nanny' used to lie *perdu* in the evenings in a certain whin-covered bank – a regular gorse covert in those days, as I was made to understand. Here these young fellows beat for her as they would for a hare, and for the same purpose – namely, for sport's sake – and expecting to find her in her *quasi* form there. When found, she always 'took the same line of country,' namely, up the hill from the side of the basin low down in which her hut was placed, and then along the slope from the moor-end down towards the hamlet called Ainthorpe, and so down the steeper part of the same descent to where a run of water used to cross the road on its surface, but is now bridged over in a substantial, if not a showy, manner. Down this steeper descent there was and is a flagged path of causey – the survival of what had once been the veritable highroad, or king's high-way, up and towards the eastern part of the parish. Down this causey it was the witch's custom, when she was thus chivied, to run at headlong speed, and as she wore clogs, or rough shoes with wooden soles, fortified at the extremities with iron tips and heels, the clatter of her footsteps could be heard long before she arrived near the foot of the slope, and the water, at which perforce the chase ceased. One evening one of the customary starters and pursuers had not been present at the 'meet', nor consequently at the 'find'. However, he was near the lower part of the causey when the clatter of the wooden shoes at the highest part warned him that the hunt was up. His first thought was to stop the quarry in her headlong race for the running water, and see what would happen when she was headed and forced to turn back, or away from her refuge. So he set himself firmly right across the causey aforesaid, with his legs necessarily a little apart, in order to stop the gangway effectually. Onwards came the chase; the footsteps sounded nearer and nearer, and sharper and sharper. But there was nothing to be seen.

Thomas P— began to be in a fright, rather: it was uncanny to hear what he heard, and as he heard it, and to know that the witch he had so often harried and hunted was the author of it, and yet not be able to see a hair of her. But he had no time for deliberation; and before he had made up his mind about the best thing to be done, he felt something rush full force between his legs, himself carried on unresistingly for a yard or two, and then hurled over on one side like a sucked orange, hearing a weird sort of chuckling laugh as the being he had expected to baffle reached the point beyond which pursuit was impracticable.

The idea in this case, as also in the story last given, was that of the witch becoming the object of pursuit, and under the form of a hare. In the one case, certainly, she spontaneously offers herself in that capacity, while in the other it hardly seems possible to assume entire willingness on her part; while, besides, there is a sort of a jumble between the silent pads of the hare[1] and the noisily resonant clatter of the iron-shod wooden clogs. But it is to be observed that the witch, under the form of a hare, is of perpetual recurrence in all the copious witch-lore of the district: most often, perhaps, as the sufferer, but by no means invariably so. And what is interesting, especially in connection with the Scandinavian repertories of the same kind, there is reference to the witch as taking that form in relation with the abstraction of milk from the cows in the field by night.

[1] There is also in this story another discrepancy or inconsistency, as collated with the ordinary witch-lore deliverances, and as regards one of their most customary features. What I refer to is the idea that the witch could not cross running water. Every one 'kens' Tam O'Shanter's adventure, and the apostrophe to his gallant mare—

> Now, do thy speedy utmost, Meg,
> An' win the key-stane of the brig;
> There at them thou thy tail may toss,
> A running stream they darena cross;

and in one of the most graphic of the witch stories known to me as told in this district, the convicted witch remains in acute suffering because she is unable to cross a stream and undo the spell which is torturing her. And yet, in this story of the hunted Nanny, her flight is always directed to the running water at Ainthorpe, once beyond which she was no longer the victim of her persecutors' malice or mischief. But this is nearly the only, if not the one single, striking incongruity of the kind that I have detected.

CHAPTER THREE

Witch Work

IT was very much otherwise with many of the 'noted witches' who had the credit of doing so much mischief that remedial measures had to be taken, shooting at them with silver shot or silver slugs seeming to be the only, at least the readiest, means available. Thus, in Glaisdale Head the trees in a young plantation were continually eaten off. If replaced, still the same fate awaited their successors. It was easy to say there was nothing new in having young sapling trees gnawed completely off by hares and rabbits; or, if of larger size, barked by the latter if not by the former. But there were circumstances in this case which showed – so it was said – that no mere ordinary hare was the cause of the damage complained of. 'Hares might have been seen in the nursery (plantation), leastwise, one particular hare, a bit off the common to look at: but common hares did not cut the tops of the young trees off, ommost as gin they had been cut wiv a whittle, and leave 'em liggin' about just as they were cut, as if nobbut for mischeef. Hares was reasonable creatur's eneough, and i' lang ho'dding-storms, when ivvery thing was deep happed wi' snow, and they could na get a bite ov owght else, they'd sneap t' young trees, and offens dee a canny bit ov ill. But they did not come, storm or nae storm, and just knipe off tweea or three score o' young saplings, any soort o' weather, as if for gam' or mischeef.' So the usual consultation was held, and with the issue that watch was to be kept by the owner concerned, with a gun loaded with silver shot – which, by the way, was procured as in the last case – and the moment he saw the suspicious hare beginning its nefarious practices, he was to take steady aim and shoot. The watch was set, and at the 'witching hour of night' of course, the hare put in an appearance – 'a great, foul au'd ram-cat ov a heear t' leuk at – and began knepping here and knepping there as if 't wur stoodying how best t' deea maist ill i' lahtlest tahm. Sae t' chap at wur watching, he oop wi's gun, and aiming steady he lat drive (discharged his gun). My wo'd! but there was a flaysome skrike!

An' t' heear, sair ho't (badly wounded), gat hersel' a soort o' croppen out o' t' no'ssery, and ho'ppled (hirpled, limped, hobbled) away as weel's she could, an' won heeam at last at Au'd Maggie's house-end, in a bit o' scroggs at grows on t' bank theear.' Inquiries however, were made next day, not among the brushwood on the bank (steep slope or hillside), but at the cottage of the old woman called 'Au'd Maggie'; and unluckily for her reputation, already more than sufficiently shaky in the witch connection, she was found in her bed 'sair ho't in many spots', she said with splinters of a broken bottle she had fallen down upon; but her visitors thought 'mair lik'ly wi' shot-coorns o' some soort'.

Another story, essentially of the same character, but varying in some of the details, runs as follows: A farmer in Farndale was terribly unlucky with his live stock. 'Stirk and heifer, yearlings and two-year-au'ds, he had lossen yan efter anither, and naebody kenned what ailed 'em; and now at last t' cauves wur gannan' too. And it had coomed to be notished that, whenivver a lahtle black bitch wur seen i' t' grip o' t' cow-'us, or i' t' cauf-pen, then, for seear, yan iv 'em took bad and dee'd.' So the customary consultation ensued, and the accustomed advice was sought, and the prescription was: 'Charge your gun with silver shot, watch for the black bitch – but be sure you don't shoot your neighbour's black cur-dog (collie) – and when it gets out of your garth, let drive.' All was arranged accordingly. The black 'female dog' came in due time; it was noted that it was black all over, off forefoot and all – the neighbour's cur-dog had that foot white; it was in the grip (the groove or channel in the floor behind the cow-stalls), but it could not win into the calves' pen; and as it was leaving the farmstead garth the fatal shot was fired, followed by the 'skrike' as aforesaid; the domiciliary visit, not of condolence but of detection, was paid next day, and the suffering witch found groaning in bed, with a terrible series of shot-wounds in the hinder part of her person.

There were other modes, besides those recorded in these stories, of bringing an offending witch to book; as there were divers offences and shades of offence alleged against the offender; but the majority of the tales did not record such eventual proof of the justice of the suspicion, or overwhelming testimony that the punishment had fallen on the actual transgressor. Indeed, in a very considerable class of stories the punishment inflicted on the particular witch proceeded against was rather left to inference than specified, or even indicated. Nay, there were even cases in which modes of permanent or sustained annoyance or mortification of the witch were resorted to; measures calculated and intended to defeat or frustrate her malice, and to nullify her power. Thus, I have before me now a spell or charm the object of which was to hamper and hinder the witch in her attempts (possible or anticipated) to injure the stock of the person employing it. And this said charm or spell was in process of application much within the period of my personal residence here and acquaintance with the said person. He was the largest farmer in the parish, a right good sort, and a fair specimen of the old untutored, unschooled Yorkshire yeoman, with a large amount of natural shrewdness at the bottom, and with any amount of credulity in some directions, and obstinate incredulity in others, mainly on the side where reason and knowledge lay. He could neither read nor write – by no means an unknown thing among the Dales farmers of fifty years ago; but he was as honest as the day – in horse-dealing even. Perhaps I need hardly say he had a lively sense of the actuality of the witch, of her power, of her malice, and not least, of the ascertained direction of it against himself and his belongings. He never assigned any reason he had for supposing himself a special object for the malevolence of the uncanny old crone. But why, or how, could he doubt it? Were not his beasts continually affected with the red-water, when his neighbours' were not? Was there ever a year when he did not lose a yearling or two, or may be more, with some mysterious languishing illness? Were not his calves afflicted above other men's calves, so that he scarcely ever was able to rear more than a part of them? Of course, to one like him, this reasoning was irrefutable, and he 'went the entire animal' in his appreciation of what the witch – whether it were one or several – could and did do day by day continually. Prejudiced people might say that bad management, insufficient food and shelter, pasturage on sour undrained lands, with an alternation of scraping for bare subsistence on dry, parched, shaly banks, might have something to do with the unluck of his stock generally; but my old friend Jonathan knew a vast better than that. 'There was more than one witch in the Head (Fryup Head), and there was more than him as kenned it.' Well, among other ways and means, Jonathan employed a standing charm; and when he died it was found in (as was to be presumed) full operation, in his standing-desk or bureau, with a white-handled penknife, half open, laid in front of it. It consisted of a half-sheet of letter-paper, folded in the fashion of those days when as yet the envelope was undiscovered, and sealed with three black seals, inserted between each two of which was a hackle from a red cock's neck. This, when opened, was found to have a pentacle, inscribed within a circle, drawn on it. It is somewhat difficult to make out which is top and which is bottom. But from such indications as there are, I assume that the point from which the passage from the Psalms, which surrounds the circle just named, begins to read is the bottom. The said extract is, 'In Him shall be the strength of thy hand. He shall keep thee in six troubles, yea, even in seven shall no harm come to thee,' – the 'thee' being interlined over the word 'come'. In the central hexagonal space formed by the mutual interesection of the three triangles which form the figure, is what is meant for a short sentence of three words in the Hebrew character, but is really a mere rough imitation, such as might be made by an ignorant impostor, who knew the general characteristics of the Hebrew as printed. There are then six triangular spaces formed by the cutting off of the apices of the composing triangles by the intersecting sides of the same; and beginning with the lowest – as we are regarding the diagram – and proceeding to the right, round the circle, in the first (or lowest) is the word 'Agla'; in the next, the letters of the word 'El'; in the third, 'On'; in the fourth, and upside down, as we are regarding it, the word 'Nalgah', with a cross above it; in the fifth, 'Adonai'; and in the sixth, 'Sadai'. Besides these triangular spaces, there are six other spaces formed by the segments of the containing circle cut off between the several apices of the constituent triangles and the sides of the small vertical triangles, already noted. Taking as the first of these that on the left of the triangular space numbered as the first, just above, the words inscribed are, 'Caro verbum factum est'; and proceeding in the same order as before, in the second the inscription is, 'Jesu Christi Nazarenus Rex Judaeorum;' in the third, the word 'Permumaiton'; in the fourth, 'Amati schema;' in the fifth, 'Sadai'; and in the sixth, 'Adonai'. Turning the charm the other way up, nearly underneath the cross above named, as it now stands, begins the sentence, 'Ye are everlasting power of God theos'; and then, at the bottom of all, in a straight line, the words 'Hoc in vince', all run together, as was the case also in the sentence previously noticed. This last, doubtless, refers directly to the sign of the cross made immediately above in the small triangle containing the word 'Nalgah.'

Surely a formidable-looking weapon of defence is here, and, as it is reasonable to suppose, one likely to occasion Jonathan's unfriends among the uncanny crew of witches more than a mere occasional miscarriage of some of their nefarious, however craftily laid, schemes and intentions.

But there were other and less elaborate, and beyond question less costly, means available for frustrating, or at least in some measure enervating, the witch's maleficent energy. I say 'less costly', because a spell like the one just described involved a visit to the nearest, or possibly the most renowned, 'wise man' (of whom more at a future page) in the district; and he, like the doctor and the lawyer and other learned professors, naturally expected and took care to secure his *honorarium, quid pro quo,* or fee.

Here a little story told me by one of my parishioners of the days that are gone, and to whose normal unwillingness to talk to me on such matters reference has been made at a previous page. The story was on this wise: He was out and about his farm one day, several of the fields belonging to which lay far up towards the Head of the dale, where the surroundings, however rugged and picturesque, were quite sufficiently lonely. Rarely indeed, when I have been – as I have been scores of times, whether with my gun or with only my walking-stick for my companion – in that part of my parish, have I ever seen a human being in these wild solitudes, except attracted by the sound of my gun, or perchance in quest of some stray sheep. Naturally, then, my old friend was a little surprised, not to say startled, at seeing one day a woman he knew, and knew as somewhat quaint in some of her ways, coming by an unfrequented route into the loneliest part of this lonely wilderness; and not only that, but casting anxious and inquiring looks all about her, as if wishing to be assured she was neither followed nor under observation. She was carrying some bright object in her hand, which, as well as he could see from the distance at which he stood, might be a 'gully', or large domestic knife. His first thought, he told me, on recognizing the female in question, and connecting her queer suspicious ways with the fact of her being in such a peculiarly lonely and, for her, strangely out-of-the-way place, was that she might be meditating making away with herself. A little consideration seemed to be sufficient to dispel that notion, and after watching her with some little wonderment for a few minutes, he went about his business. A little later in the day he met her full face, and apparently bending her steps towards her own home. But the way she was pursuing involved a considerable circuit, as leading from the place at which he had last seen her, and particularly as connected with the route by which she had entered on the scene when he had noticed her. 'Hie, Hannah,' he said to her, 'what mak'st t' here? – 'Wheea,' says she, 'An's just gannan' yam (home) t' gainest (nearest) way Ah can.' And then he told her he thought it was a strange sort of 'gainest way home' for her to be taking, considering where he had seen her an hour or so before, and the way he had seen her arrive there by. And then he went on to tell her how her goings on had perplexed him, and how for a minute or two he had thought perhaps he ought to follow her, and prevent her doing herself a mischief. The poor woman seemed a little taken aback by the discovery that she had been thus under observation, when she had fondly imagined that all her doings were unseen, at least unnoted by any mortal eye; but presently, recovering herself, she uttered the explanatory sentence, 'Wheea, I was nobbut lating my witch-wood' (only seeking my wood-charm against witches). Well, but why go all the way into the Head, and that far into the Head, moreover? In reply to this, and a series of other questions, the old woman gave the following mass of information: To be effectual, the requisite pieces of rowan-tree – for many were wanted: one for the upper sill of the house-door, one for the corresponding position as to stable, cow-byre, and the other domiciles of the various stock, one for personal use, one for the head of her bed, one for the house-place, etc. etc., – must not only be cut on St. Helen's day, but, in order to be quite fully efficacious, they must be cut with a household knife: they must be cut, moreover, from a tree which not only the cutter had never seen before, but of the very existence of which he must have had no previous knowledge or suspicion; and that, on the tree having been found in this blindfold sort of way, and the requisite bough or boughs having been severed and secured, they must be carried home by any way save that by which the obtainer of them had gone forth on his quest. And so, as she had known all the rowan-trees in the nearer neighbourhood of her cottage for years, she had been obliged to go farther afield, and all her proceedings had been regulated according to these various conditions.

Whether these conditions were always and punctiliously observed by the devout believers in the power of the witch and in the prophylactic efficacy of the witch-wood, I am not able from positive knowledge or information to affirm; but I am quite well aware that the consumption of the article in question was by no means small, and that, too, even within the period of my personal acquaintance with the district.

But there were other means of anticipating or obviating such harm and loss, and not a few, besides these already mentioned. Thus, I knew an old lady, a dear, canny old body she was, who, before she proceeded to churn, invariably took forcible measures to expel the witch, or any witch-emissary, who might, in the malice of her intention, have lodged herself in the churn. And this she did by proceeding to throw one pinch of salt into the fire and another into the churn, repeating the alternate sprinkling until the mystic number of nine times for each had been completed. Another and not ineffectual method on the like occasion was – in order, I suppose, to make the place too hot to hold the witch – to take the kitchen poker, heated to an unmistakable red heat, and, inserting it at the opening or bung-hole, to turn it slowly round, sweeping as wide a space as possible within the said utensil, nine several times. Witch-wood too had its allotted station in the dairy, and in connection with the various dairy vessels.

What a jolly life I used to think the little village boys who were set to 'keep the crows' in that then wheat-growing county of Essex must lead. No tiresome school, dame or boarding, no multiplication table, or, worse still, pence-table, to learn, no work of any kind – for bird-nesting and cutting the bark off long switches in alternate rings clearly was not work – but just to halloa *ad libitum* from time to time when the crows might be coming, or the master or the foreman be within hearing – and what boy does not like kicking up a hullabaloo of that kind when it suits him? – but over and above all the rest, and over and above with a towering pre-eminence, the privilege and the opportunity to fire the real gun, and then to recharge it one's own glorified self! Certainly, creeping round those huge thirty- or forty-acre fields, and duly peeping into every fork in the old thick hedge, and scrutinizing every moss-covered stub, and every half-hidden but suggestive hollow in the bank, all took time, and when you were doing your 'work' of this kind on one side of the wide field, the crows might perchance find their way in at the other, and pick up a few stray grains of the scattered seed-corn. Again, sitting down and ringing those bonny long straight sticks required a good deal of attention and care, and even measurement, and when one was intent on such rightful occupation, of course a cunning, cautious, keen-eyed crow might seize the chance afforded by such pre-occupation. Besides, a boy, even a brazen-throated one, cannot always be halloaing, especially on market-days or sales-days, when both master and looker are safe to be away, 'minding their business' there.

Lastly, too, the gunpowder is dealt out in such graduated doses, like physic that is not bad to take, that you cannot in the nature of things keep up an all-day-long fusillade, and so, some way or other, the crows that our small friends in rough boots which smell of stale oil, and ragged jackets that tell of past rather than future wear, are set 'to keep', find as many loopholes as a rabbit in the fence enclosing its natural covert, or as the proverbial coach-and-six in the proverbial Act of Parliament.

'Ay, the witch might have – there's not yan that kens, but kens that she *had* – a vast o' power; but the Wise Man he had a vast mair; he was mair 'an a maister over sike as her.'

And great was the resort by our old friend Jonathan, and many and many another of his day and school, to the said Wise Man on the occurrence of troubles of the class and kind indicated. And, as became a wise man, many and various were the resources at his command; but, being a wise man, he did not take everything for granted, even when related with a strange quaint fulness of detail, enforced by a heap of stranger imaginations and more marvellous amplifications of suspicions as to person and motive. 'Ay, maybe your beasts are "witched". What you tell me looks like it. And Au'd Betty may be at the bottom of it. She's a noted witch – we all ken that. And as like as not she has a bit of a grudge against you. Nay, even if it bean't as bad as that, still some folks can't keep themselves quiet, even if they'd like. They mun be doing, or him that gies them the power might not be weel suited. Still, ye ken, we mun be canny, and ken what we're efter. I mak' no doubt that somebody has "witched" your stock, and maybe "wished you" (invoked some evil thing upon you) as well. But that is what we have got to find out. And if we mak' sure o' that, why then we'll see who's done it.' Some discourse of this kind, there is no doubt, passed between the Wise Man and the seeker unto him. And one not uncommon recipe furnished by him – for a consideration always; that goes with-out saying – was as follows, due instructions as to time and mode of provision of the requisites named being first of all given: 'Take nine bottry (boretree, common elder) knots, and put them on a clean platter all close together, but without too much care about arranging them in regular order; only let them be all in a bunch. Then cover them – exactly at midnight is the right time – cover them with a clean cloth, set the whole on a table near the window, and take tent that no one goes nigh-hand them while (until) the morning. And if, when you take the cloth off in the morning, you find them all squandered (scattered in confusion) about the platter, well, it's a safe thing that your stock is really witched.' Then, in some cases, especially if the symptoms were not very urgent, came a further inquiry as to the identity of the wrong-doing hag, who was the active cause of the trouble in hand. But in cases of emergency, where the stock was grievously afflicted, and perhaps death was already busy among them, more summary measures were resorted to, and without delay. One course, of which I heard from more informants than one, and which I had unquestionable reasons for being assured had been put in practice, twice if not three times, by the Jonathan mentioned above during his occupation of the farm he held in this parish, was much if not exactly as follows: He took the heart of one of the animals which had died under the malevolent witch's maleficent practices, and having provided himself with all the various requisites, proceeded to stick it carefully with nine new pins, nine new needles, and nine new nails. Then a fire was to be made as the 'holl time of the night' (the depth of the night) drew on, yet not with ordinary or any haphazard kind of fuel; but with bottree wood – in one or two of the stories rowan-tree wood, or even ash-wood, was specified – and such wood only was to be used. And the fire was to be kindled and kept up so that there might be the hottest possible bed of bright, clear-burning embers exactly at midnight. But before lighting the fire all the doors and windows of the house were to be made fast, very safely fast; and besides, the utmost care had to be taken to darken the windows, and even cover the cracks in the door (if there were any), so that no ray of light should by any possibility be seen from the outside, and no curious eye from without be able to penetrate to the mysteries within. And on no account, whatever happened, whatever noise or disturbance occurred without, was any one to look out or do anything to interfere with the precautionary barriers against external observation or interference. All this duly attended to, the prepared heart was to be placed on the glowing bed prepared for it at just such time that it might be dried to a coal and ready to take fire, and blaze away and fall into ashes, at the very hour of midnight; at which precise moment two verses of a certain psalm were to be read aloud by the principal operator. On one occasion when this uncanny ceremonial was carried out to the very letter, the concomitant circumstances outside, according to the statement of the narrator, were more than sufficiently startling; and he told me with all the apparent simplicity and sincerity of a person who believed it all himself, and had no sort of doubt he was telling an 'ower true tale.' He described the house and its situation to me, with all the circumstances of local feature and character. It was a house with a door in the front, there being the parlour on one side and the 'house' or living-room on the other, into which, moreover, the door opened. Between it and a roadway which ran past it lay a bit of garden-ground separated from the roadway by railings, through which a wicket-gate gave admission to a flagged pathway leading directly to the door just now mentioned. As the witching hour drew on, cries and moans as of one in pain were heard outside. As the heart began to shrivel and blacken, these increased in intensity. As it began to blaze, and the reader commenced the reading prescribed, steps as of a person shod with the wooden clogs of the district, iron-tipped and iron-heeled, clattered loudly down the flags, – a loud lumbering noise was heard as of heavy wheelbarrows driven hastily over a pavement of cobble-stones, unearthly efforts such as might have been made by some boneless and yielding body, against the barred and darkened doors and windows, and then, just as the heart blazed up with a final leap of flame and collapsed into darkening ashes, a prolonged wail, like that of one in bitter agony, and after that only still silence.

In another case, all the details of which were given me with even minute exactness, embracing the names and residences of witch and victim, the mischiefs enacted, the mode of conviction employed, the scene of the final ordeal – all appertaining to the neighbouring parish of Westerdale – the new pins, new nails, new needles, nine of each again, were to be put into a clean bottle, which was then to be very securely corked, so that by no ordinary means could the cork be extracted; and then it was to be buried in a hole dug for the purpose with much secrecy, and not without due observance and ceremony, and, besides that, on the other side of a small stream which ran along the foot of the steep bank on the side of which the spell-detected witch's rudely and anciently fashioned hut-cottage stood; and buried, moreover, with the neck and cork downwards, the filling in of the hole being very carefully done, and all made as like an undisturbed bit of ground as could be. The witch – no other, in fact, than the old carline who had changed her shape into that of a hare, as detailed in a former narrative – soon began to feel the effects of the spell laid upon her, then began to be sorely uneasy, tried all her arts, all her power, to reverse it or make it of none effect; but all in vain. Indeed, she ascertained what the spell was, and where in its sensible potency it was acting; but though she was able actually to move the bottle in its mysterious hiding-place, she could not reverse it, or tamper with the security of the cork, or in the least degree impair the efficacy of the charm. At last, in the extremity of her suffering, which was becoming more than she could bear, she wandered down to the place where the bottle was hid, regardless of the implied confession, at least disclosure, of her guiltiness, with the intent of doing by manual agency what she found herself unable to do by aid of witchcraft – namely, tear the bottle out of its hole. And then came in the power of the running water, and the superior craft of the Wise Man, who had been duly consulted, and under whose direction every one of the preceding steps had been taken. She could not cross the running stream! There, within arms reach of the active instrument of her pitiful misery, she was remediless and helpless altogether. Just then as previously instructed by the doughty discoverer of witches, the sufferer under her malice and unhallowed practices enters on the scene. A short colloquy ensues, the issue of which is that the witch, in the extremity of personal suffering, surrenders unconditionally, reverses her evil spells, and promises to undo all the mischief then in progress, and never to injure him and his again. The victim of her spells then proceeds to take up the bottle out of the hole, and finds it, of course through the potency of the spells the unlucky witch had exercised in her desperate efforts to medicine her pains, almost drawn up to the surface of the ground, and thinks to himself he has had but a narrow escape after all. The sequel of the story is that he breaks the bottle, and so dissolves the charm, and the poor suffering, baffled hag obtains relief and escapes with her life, which had come in sore danger through what the Wise Man had laid upon her.

CHAPTER FOUR

The Wise Man

I DO not know how it may be with others, but to me, when thinking over such legends and narratives as those above given, it appears that the conception of the Wise Man is not only extraordinary, but also exceptional and anomalous – himself a wizard, and the chief of witches, and yet the foe of witches, the counter-plotter and confounder of the whole malignant crew. That the conception is a very old one, as old, or nearly as old, as that of the witch herself, it is hardly necessary to remind ourselves. But there are other matters in the conception which call for a measure of attention. The witch was supposed to derive her power more or less directly from the evil spirit himself. The Wise Man, however, was scarcely credited with commerce with 'T' au'd un', either personally or indirectly. The witch again was credited with malignity more or less pronounced. Not so the Wise Man, but rather the reverse. The one went about not exactly like a roaring lion seeking his prey, but still seeking victims, some to maltreat, injure, and destroy; others of whom an evil-gotten gain might accrue. The other stayed at home to be consulted, and always ready for a consideration to do the good he was asked to do. And yet this jelly-fish sort of beneficence and benevolence was scarcely assumed by the devotees, or even too forcibly declared by the Wise Man himself, to · be altogether celestial in its origin, any more than it was purely unselfish in its application and utility. I look upon the conception of the Wise Man as a survival, and a survival only – that is to say, as I found it still extant here some forty odd years ago. And, like other survivals, it had both lost and gained in divers particulars. The conception in reality would seem to be a compound arising out of a confusion of the characters and credentials of three or four original creations of the imagination, aided by overtrow and superstition. In other words, I think the Wise Man part wizard or witch, part sorcerer, magician, or enchanter, and part 'conjurer' in the true and full sense of the word. But I think there was more of the

THE WISE MAN 53

conjurer, and of the sorcerer and enchanter, in him than of the wizard or witch. And if any one tries, he will find it harder than perhaps he anticipated to keep these characters and their special attributes apart in the character under notice. Perhaps some illustration of this position may be obtained by collation of the two following quotations from Brand. Grose says, 'A sorcerer or magician differs from a witch in this: a witch derives all her power from a compact with the Devil; a sorcerer commands him and the infernal spirits by his skill in powerful charms and invocations; and also soothes and entices them by fumigations.' The difference between a conjurer, a witch, and an enchanter, according to Minshew, on the other hand, is as follows: 'The conjurer seemeth by praiers and invocations of God's powerful names to compell the Divell to saie or doe what he commandeth him. The witch dealeth rather by a friendly and voluntarie conference or agreement between him (or her) and the Divell or familiar, to have his (or her) turn served, in lieu or stead of blood or other gift offered unto him, especially of his (or her) soule. And both these differ from inchanters or sorcerers, because the former two have personall conference with the Divell, and the other meddles not with medicines and ceremonial forms of words called charmes, without apparition.' The confusion is manifest. The character and some of the attributes of the witch are fairly distinct and clear, however vague and blurred, as well as imperfectly delineated, the general character may be. But can anything like that be said as to the ideas or conceptions of the conjurer and the sorcerer? And surely the fundamental idea in the word conjurer – one whose tools or implements, material instruments of operation, are invocations, exorcisms, spells or forms of words instinct with power – is totally different from that involved in the word magician or enchanter; one, that is, who works by the exercise of occult arts, magic arts, the black art, or whatever other name may be, or may have been, applied to his supposed supernatural enginery.

But I am in danger of being led away from the Cleveland conception of the Wise Man of less than a hundred years ago. I have heard much of him, and, as I suppose, the ideal of him is preserved in the hundred and one stories told of 'Au'd Wreeghtson, t' Wahse man o' Stowsley.' And in all the stories I have heard of him, and whoever chanced to be the narrator, I never once heard him spoken of as a man of mischief, or as an evil-liver, or as extortionate, or as a man who had, it was likely or possible, made a compact with the devil; or even as one with whom the less people had to do the better. No doubt, by some he was spoken of with a kind of involuntary or unconscious awe; and by all he was evidently credited with the possession of extraordinary insight, knowledge, and power.

More than one or two of the most remarkable and the most graphic of the stories I used to listen to came from one who had himself visited the Wise Man of Stokesley. He was the man to whom pointed reference was made at an earlier page, a good, sensible, simple-minded old man, who had up to quite recently held an office of trust and much responsibility, when I obtained from him the details about to be given. And I would observe that the terms employed by him in speaking of Wrightson were simply terms of respect, not unmingled with a sort of wondering awe. And certainly nothing that I heard either from him or any other of my informants was such as to prepare me to read such a notice of him as that which is conceived in the following terms. The narrator, it should be said, is described as a Yorkshire gentleman, and the date given is 1819. 'Impostors who feed and live on the superstitions of the lower orders are still to be found in Yorkshire. These are called Wise Men, and are believed to possess the most extraordinary power in remedying all diseases incidental to the brute creation, as well as the human race; to discover lost or stolen property, and to foretell future events. One of these wretches was a few years ago living at Stokesley in the North Riding of Yorkshire; his name was John Wrightson, and he called himself the seventh son of a seventh son, and professed ostensibly the calling of a cow-doctor ('cow-leech', it should have been). To this fellow people whose education, it might have been expected, would have raised them above such weakness, flocked; many came to ascertain the thief, when they had lost any property; others for him to cure themselves or their cattle of some indescribable complaint. Another class visited him to know their future fortunes; and some to get him to save them from being balloted into the militia, – all of which he professed himself able to accomplish. All the diseases which he was sought to remedy he invariably imputed to witchcraft, and although he gave drugs which have been known to do good, yet he always enjoined some incantation to be observed, without which he declared they could never be cured. This was sometimes an act of the most wanton barbarity,[1] as

---

[1] In all my many inquiries and all my continued listenings I never heard one single syllable leading me to suppose, or even to suspect, anything of this kind. Had the charge been true, I must have heard of it – at least have met with some trace or evidence, however

that of roasting a game-cock alive, etc. The charges of this man were always extravagant; and such was the confidence in his skill and knowledge, that he had only to name any person as a witch, and the public indignation was sure to be directed against the poor unoffending creature for the remainder of her life' (Brand's *Popular Antiquities*, vol. iii. p. 34).

My own view of this statement is that much of it is exaggeration, and no small proportion of it gratuitous misrepresentation. My old friend John Unthank did not speak of Wrightson in such a way as this; and the story of the extravagant fees is, on the face of it, absurd. He did not do what he was asked to do for nothing, undoubtedly; but anybody who knows the country and the people, and their means, and the saving, thrifty[1] life they lead, knows that the payments actually made to professional men, parsons, lawyers, and doctors, even down to the middle of the present century (and in some cases even still), are such as to laugh that part of the statement to scorn. I have known men personally whose clerical stipends had not exceeded £40 a year at the earlier date alleged, and the medical and legal fees were in strict accordance therewith. But, quite apart from all this, the impression I was unconsciously led on to receive of Wrightson was – setting aside the inevitable circumstance

---

[1] Perhaps I might as well mention an anecdote in illustration of this point here as defer it to a future page. On occasion of the first show of live stock held under the auspices of the Danby Agricultural Association, two among the elders of the people, each much respected both in the parish and out of it, were among the after-dinner speakers. Both delivered themselves sensibly and well, and both with more than a mere touch of native humour. One of them, by name William Hartas, was an old Quaker, whose judgement, experience, and probity were equally well known, and caused him frequently to be appealed to as arbiter in cases of dispute or valuation. Among other things pithily and tersely – albeit a little quaintly – said, he addressed some remarks to the subject of, as he conceived, the apparent declension of habits of thriftiness and careful, not to say rigid, economy. He said, and I wish I could give it in his own inimitable Yorkshire, 'I aim (think, assume, believe) folks are not so saving and careful as they used to be. You must look to it. Farmers' daughters are not content with good calico, but want something smarter for their dresses; and dressing and dairying won't go together, no ways you can frame it. And the young chaps, why, they're almost as bad as the lasses; they want cloth trowsers and smart waistcoats. Why, when I was a lad there was a vast still sitting in their fathers' leather breeches, and more than one I kenned had breeks their grandfathers had had for their best, and there was a vast o' good wear in 'em yet. Mak' things last what they will, is my advice to this meeting; and old-fashioned homespun and good leather brecks is baith very lasty.'

---

slight. But I never did, and I entirely doubt the accuracy of 'this deponent'; and not in respect of this particular statement only. Both the next succeeding allegations require much more to prove that they are true than the fact that they are thus made.

that, like all others of his class, he was, up to a given degree, a charlatan and an impostor – that of a man of a not unkindly nature, with a pungent flavour of rough humour about him, shrewd and observant, and with wonderfully well-devised and well-employed means of information at his command. I say 'a charlatan and an impostor up to a certain degree'; but by no means an impostor *pur et simple*. A grudging admission that he 'gave drugs which have been known to do good' is made in the extract given above. By the light of what I think I may say I know, I should read that thus: he possessed, in common with many others then and since, wide and deep acquaintance with herbs and simples, and he used his knowledge with skill and judgement. No doubt also he knew the properties and uses of what we more usually speak of as 'drugs', and employed them accordingly. No doubt either that he possessed the power of influencing men's minds and imaginations, and knew it right well, and used it of set purpose and intention; and heightened it, moreover, by the mystic means he had at his command, and knew how to render serviceable on occasion and with sufficient impressiveness. But, grant these particulars frankly, it must yet be admitted that he had much and effectual machinery available, other than what is implied when we style a man a 'rank impostor'. The unjust steward's lord 'commended' him for the sharpness or cleverness of his trick, detected though it was. I am sure that the attitude of my mind when I had heard what Unthank had to tell me about his own personal intercourse with Wrightson (after I had heard so much about him and his doings from others) was something of the same sort as that with which the lord of the steward is accredited in the parable. I said to myself, This Wise Man must have been, no doubt, part knave; but all the same one of the cleverest, not to say ablest, fellows of his craft.[1] He must have known the district as if it were a map, and the people in it as the master knows his scholars. He must have had channels of information such that he could depend upon what they supplied him with, and yet such as not to be known, or even suspected. That some of these sources or origins of information were local, I have no doubt at all; that some of them were simply personal I have as little; and that some of them depended on confederates I regarded as established. But his confederates were they of his own household: namely, as described to

---

[1] Except Dawson, mentioned in the popular talk as Wrightson's nephew as well as successor, I have heard of no other local wise man *by name*. That there had been many another before him goes without saying. But he was as the sun among stars.

me, an elderly housekeeper-servant and an odd man about the house. I have been told too that an ostler at one of the inns at Stokesley was an ally. And there was a code of signals whereby much general information about a visitor and the cause of his application might be and was given to the master, without any personal passages between himself and his dependants. But all this will possibly be better illustrated after producing one or more of the stories to which reference has been made at an earlier page.

One of the most telling of these narratives, and possibly the most illustrative of them all, was that told me by old John Unthank. At the time of the occurrence of the incident he was living with his uncle, who held the post of gamekeeper to the then Viscount Downe, and lived at what was then called Dawnay, but now Danby, Lodge. The uncle held some pasture land of his lordship, and kept sundry cows and other stock. Among these was a beast (a stot or bullock) grievously afflicted with some mysterious disorder – an 'indescribable complaint', as the above extract phrases it. The symptoms were altogether unusual, the sufferings of the poor brute seemed to be very great, and no local cow-leech was able to make anything of the case, or hold out any prospect of cure. So the uncle decided to apply to the Wise Man, and sent his nephew to Stokesley, a ride of about eleven miles over a rough, wild, lonely road, the greater part of it. Unthank went as directed, and on reaching Stokesley proceeded first to stable his nag at one of the 'publics' there, and this done repaired to the Wise Man's abode. After some little delay he was admitted. The Wise Man was seated in his consulting room, dressed in some sort of long robe or gown, girded round him with a noticeable girdle, and with a strange-looking head-covering on. There were some of the accustomed paraphernalia of the character assumed and its pretensions – a skull, a globe, some mysterious-looking preparations, dried herbs, etc. etc. Unthank, who was then quite a young man, and to whom a journey to Stokesley formed an epoch in life, and who knew but little indeed of what went on in the world outside the lonely, half-inaccessible dale which was his home-place, was naturally impressed alike by the strange garb and the 'strange objects, and by his preconceived ideas of the personage he beheld. Before he had time, or perhaps presence of mind, to open the cause of his coming and explain what he wanted, Wrightson addressed him with the words, 'Well, John, thou's come to ask me about Tommy Frank's black beast, that is carried on in yon strange way.' Unthank told me he was taken quite aback by this unexpected greeting, and was too astounded to be ready with a word in reply; and without giving him time to collect his ideas, the Wise Man went on – 'Why, it is little use your coming to me for advice, or to ask me for something to mend the beast, if I can't tell you why you've come, and what you want. And maybe you think I can't do that. But I'll let you see that I ken more than you think. What was it the last thing your uncle said to you before you left to ride to Stokesley?' Unthank told me he stopped a moment to recollect, and before he had recalled the parting words, Wrightson continued, 'Ay, I see you have forgotten. But I'll tell you. The last thing he said to you was, "Now, John, you mind and see t' galloway gets her whoats and eats 'em afore you leaves t' stable." ' 'And, by gum,' said the old man to me, 'them was the very words my uncle said to me as I rode away out of the yard.' Wrightson then went on to tell his visitor divers particulars touching the sick animal. He described the position it occupied in the cow-byre – the door opened right on to its rump, only a much coarser word was employed; it made a very peculiar and unusual noise; it was continually shifting its position; the spasms or fits of pain came on at such and such times, and the manifestations were variable, and so forth. It was all accurate and true, and Unthank seemed to think he could not have told the Wise Man about the beast so clearly and descriptively as Wrightson had told him. The end of the interview was that Wrightson said he could do nothing that would be of any good; that the affection under which the beast was suffering was past his skill; that the poor beast would die; and that when it was dead, they had better open it – in politer language, hold a post-mortem examination – and then they would find some abnormal growth which was the cause of the illness and pain, and would be, with scarce any delay, the cause of the death. Unthank further stated that when the beast died it was opened accordingly, that the strange growth inside was found, and, in fact, that everything the Wise Man had said was verified.

Now, I have no hesitation in admitting that I believed the story as the old man told it me from point to point. He told it with great clearness, and as he went on with it seemed almost to be living the scene over again. He grew quite animated, and told it all with readiness and fluency as if it had been something he had witnessed but a day or two before. And besides believing it to be an essentially true story, I thought I could see the explanation of much which seemed the most striking, and which at the time had, to Unthank himself, seemed the most startling.

It was, of course, a piece of Wrightson's business, nay, of his very 'wisdom', to keep himself *au courant* of all such extraordinary cases as this. His system of information, well organized, as I have already said I think it must have been, would provide him with early notices of all such matters; and his code of home signals would acquaint him with much that remained to be known. Given that he had a canny old house-keeper and an inquiring man about the house, and an ally at the inn stables, there would be no great difficulty in fishing out of the compara-tive novice, as Unthank was, such minor matters as the position of the creature in the byre even, and much more the general way in which it was 'handled', or 'carried on'; and even the parting caution of old Tommy Frank, whose peculiarities, moreover, were well known to less shrewd and observant people than the Wise Man himself, was one which might easily have been forecasted.

Another characteristic story which I had from Unthank, as also an independent counterpart from my other great informant in such matters, was given me with great precision of detail, as well as with the names, families, and abodes of the actors – or rather the acted upon – in the transaction as described. Two men, both belonging to, or at least connected with, this parish, were on their way to Stokesley on some particular occasion, – the 'Hirings' there, I think I am right in assuming, – when it occurred to one of them, just as they were going down the bank or steep moor-side, lying above the West House – a singularly lonely farm on the road from Castleton to Stokesley, and within a mile or so of Kildale – to propose to the other, as his idea of a joke – 'Let's gan and have a bit o' spoort wiv Au'd Wreeghtson.' They were to go to him as if in earnest, with some imaginary case, I forget what, even if it was mentioned in the narrative; but his wisdom was to be tested by asking his advice about a matter which existed in imagination rather than in reality. In due time they reached his house, and were before long admitted into his presence. But there was no long robe or head-gear with mystic symbols; no grinning skull or stuffed creatures of strange or gruesome look. The sage was in the houseplace, with his pipe in his mouth, sitting in his own comfortable high-backed chair, with a cheery fire – for it was Martinmas time, when the days are raw and cold – and with something to drink quite handy. The Wise Man made his visitors kindly welcome, made them draw in their chairs to the fire, provided them with pipes and tobacco, and no doubt the requisite moisture also, and, in short, 'behaved hissel' real menseful wiv 'em'.

The day was cold, and he heaped on fuel, and kept them 'weel enter-tained wi' pross an' talk'. Presently, as the fire began to blaze up higher and higher, and the glow to become ruddier and hotter, the visitors began to find they were over near the glowing coals for comfort, and they were for setting their seats a bit back. But try as they would, not only the said seats would not move, but they themselves were quite fast in their seats! The heat continued to become more and more unbearable, and what with the roasting they were getting, and the perturbation of spirit which had come upon them on realizing their position, they were undergoing the experience of the inner fat of the newly-slaughtered pig when being 'rendered' (melted down) in the process of conversion into lard. After quietly enjoying their discom-fiture and their discomfort for a space, and when nature could have endured no further continuance of melting moments such as theirs, Wrightson quietly but sardonically said to them, 'Ay, ye cam' to ha'e a bit o' spoort wiv Au'd Wreeghtson. Au'd Wreeghtson aims it's a spoort 'at differs fra what ye considered (settled on, fixed) coming down West House bank. Anither tahm, mebbe, ye'll think tweea tahms afore making spoort wiv Au'd Wreeghtson. And noo, Gude deea tiv ye!' and as he spoke those last words, they found themselves freed from their previous helplessness, and losing no time in elaborate leave-takings, they got themselves away from the uncomfortable presence of such a joker as 't' Wahse Man o' Stowsley.'

Here again, with all the features of a very uncanny insight into men's thoughts and intentions, it seems to me by no means impossible to give an intelligible account of the whole affair. Thus, it is hardly possible to think of a couple of young men, bent on a spree of the kind in question, keeping their scheme religiously secret. It is far more likely that, whether with a sort of bravado, or with an idea of the great original wit involved in their purpose, they would talk about their intention, and the where and when and how of its original conception. And as to the fixing them in their chairs, the simple supposition that he possessed certain so called mesmeric powers – a supposition that ac-credits itself as soon as suggested – is enough to account for it, and there certainly would be nothing marvellous in an experiment of that description.

But still, there are other stories about this personage and his doings, the explanation of which must be of an entirely different cast – namely, that we have a good deal of embellishment, addition, exaggeration, perhaps even fiction, connected with them. Certainly these were told me by my two principal and most trustworthy informants with the same amount of apparent faith, often assuming the aspect of thorough conviction, as any of their other recollections or experiences. But then there were elements in them which claimed a very confiding receptiveness, or a very well grown credulity, in order to accept them all, chapter and verse, just as they were told. One of these was touching the recovery of some stolen weights, and another, of the same general character, as to the recovery of a stolen shirt. Perhaps I ought to state at once that, according to the legends I had so many occasions to listen to, no small part, and, no doubt, the most lucrative part of the Wise Man's 'practice' seems to have been connected with the recovery of stolen or otherwise lost goods. Indeed, that is one of the items in the indictment laid in the extract from Brand. The stories I specially refer to were on this wise. The weights belonging to one of water-mills on the Esk in this parish were found one fine morning to be missing and it was at once concluded that they had been stolen. After vain search and inquiry, a messenger was sent to the Wise Man. On his arrival, and after giving in his information, and answering all the questions put to him by the wizard, he was told to go straight home, and, it was added, 'Thee'll find the weights back again afore thou wins sae far, and they'll be all clamed wiv (with) ass-muck,' – in other words, smeared over with peat-ashes and such other refuse as is thrown into an ordinary moorland ash-pit. And the final direction was, 'Thee'd best not ask any questions. Ah kens all about it, and when thee gets t' weights back, thee'll be nane the warse. Sae, just ho'd yer noise (make no outcry) about the matter.'[1]

The other story was of a like nature. A man living at Danby End was engaged as one of the miners employed at the Fryup Head (or Fryup Trough) coal-pits, the said pits being more than four miles

[1] By the kind permission of Sir Joseph Whitwell Pease, I add the following story, belonging to the same class with this just told, and which he narrates himself: 'As to old Wreeghtson, I recollect my grandfather telling several stories about him. Some hams belonging to his mother, hanging in the wool warehouse at Darlington, were stolen. The mill-hands were much disturbed lest any of them should be suspected. They sent a deputation to the Wise Man at Stowsley, the members of it necessarily staying the night there. They saw the Wise Man, who said, "Them that's gotten the hams is tired of them: they'll be fund before you get back to Darnton." They left Stokesley at daybreak, arriving at Darlington at dinner-time (noon). The mill-hands were crossing the bridge over the dam when, just as the ambassadors arrived, one of the workmen saw the mistresses's hams in the water. No doubt the dread of discovery by the supernatural wisdom of the Wise Man had alarmed the thief.'

from his house. A wilder scene can hardly be imagined; the Trough being a ravine, and the pits themselves in the midst of the brown, almost trackless expanse of the moor, with no human dwelling within almost half an hour's walk. The miners had a difficult time of it, as the coal is not only inferior and impure, and of but small value compared with the coal of commerce, but it is in such thin seams as to make the winning of it a matter of no small labour in proportion to the mass won. A seam of fully eighteen inches in thickness is, I should say, almost a thing unknown. Consequently the miners have to work a great amount of the adjacent strata to spoil, in order to obtain room in which to work the coal itself. A man can scarcely work in less space than four feet from floor to roof; and thus the labour is made additionally burdensome. Necessarily the men undress before descending into the pits, which, however, are none of them of any great depth. The man of whom the present story is told had left his clothes above ground as usual, but on coming to bank again he missed his shirt. All inquiry proving fruitless, he made up his mind to go directly away from the pit-mouth to Stokesley, in order to consult the Wise Man about his loss, and the possible recovery of the abstracted garment. He went off accordingly, was admitted after the usual manner, detailed his loss and the circumstances of it, answered the various interrogatories put to him, and in due course was told to go straight back home as directly as he could, and to rest comforted with the assurance that the shirt would be safely in his wife's hands before he got back himself. And then came the customary rider: 'You may think it strange I know more about this shirt than you do yourself; but if I didn't know that, and a vast more like it, it would be to no use you and such as you coming to me to find how to get back what you have lost, or maybe what folks have thieved from you. Well, I'll tell you this about your shirt; it was made by a left-handed woman. And I'll tell you one thing more. When you get home, you tell your wife not to give salt out of the house to anybody, unless she wishes the witches about to get sair ho'd on her.'

The man went home as directed, found that the shirt had, as the Wise Man had said it would, got home before him and that it was a fact that the seamstress who had made it actually was a left-handed work-woman. This put him in mind of the Wise Man's injunction about the salt, and the danger of giving it away from the house. 'Who's been here to-day?' he inquired. 'Well, nobbut so-and-so, and t' strange chap as brought the shirt, and wad say nought about it but that a man had gi'en it him to hug (carry, bear as a parcel or package) on to me.' – 'What, no one else? no one of the neighbours?' – 'Wheea, au'd Elsie Green wur in, axing me to lend her a bit o' salt, as she said she wur out' (had none left). We can imagine the rest, and one might venture to conclude that the wife, on hearing the husband's story, would not be too easy in her mind at thinking of what she had unwittingly done, and the possible consequences of the gift so unwisely bestowed.

But our very attempt to imagine all this very possibly goes part of the way in illustrating the process of mind in the thief himself in either of the cases just detailed, or indeed in any like case whatsoever. The Wise Man's commonly believed-in marvellous insight into hidden or obscure matters, the country-side persuasion that there was scarce ought but what he knew, the reputation he had, and which it is perfectly evident, from what I have called the 'riders' to these narratives, it was his object to consolidate and keep as well as obtain, must, in the very great proportion of cases, have affected the thief's mind, and powerfully too, when once he knew that the inquiry into the theft and as to the perpetrator of it had been referred to such a detective; and in quite as pronounced a manner and degree as the telling of this miner's tale and experience would affect his wife's imagination, would it impress the many neighbours to whom the narrative, and very likely with ever-increasing accentuation, came to be in due course repeated; and the thief must at once feel that detection was inevitable, and that his best plan would be to restore the plunder, and, if in such a way as to avoid exposure, so much the better. And no doubt this was one reason why the Wise Man so often enjoined a 'calm sough' about the offence and the offender upon those who went to consult him. No doubt, too, the wizard's domestic confederates would easily contrive to fish out of such people as the miller in the one case, and the miner in the other, the main points of the matters which had brought them over to consult the 'master'. It is even quite supposable that Wrightson might have become acquainted with the circumstance of there being a left-handed seamstress in some sort of connection with the shirt-loser's female belongings.

But still, when we get beyond these considerations, we are at a standstill as to any probable or reasonable hypothesis. The salt incident can only be explained away. Was the incident one of real occurrence at all? Or was it a telling addition to a tale in other respects really founded on fact? Such suggestions will present themselves, and it is impossible to avoid the conviction that they are quite reasonable and fairly satis-factory. And the story of the recovered mill-weights may perhaps be dealt with upon the same principle.

But there is yet another solution possible with a case presenting such features as these. What I mean is that the whole affair might have been a 'put-up' concern. Wrightson might have planned it, arranging all the details in such a way as to lead on to the desired result – that is to say, increased *prestige* accruing to himself. Such an assumption would explain every detail given; but I must admit that, to myself, it is utterly and entirely unsatisfactory. And certainly I never heard of any such insinuation being made against the man's doings. On the contrary, the faith in their reality as well as authenticity was a robust faith; and it would have been but to little purpose to suggest to either of my principal 'contributors' any doubt as to the *bonâ fide* nature of the things they told about the Wise Man's exploits, however strange and marvellous they may have been.

Before taking final leave of the Wise Man and his doings, I will add only the following copy, made *verbatim et literatim*, with the capitals and stops (or the want of them) precisely as in the original, or a pre-scription or recipe to be followed or put in practice in the case of an animal affected with some mysterious kind of malady, which formula is in my possession, and is, as I have reason to believe, in Wrightson's own handwriting. It is written on a half-sheet of letter-paper, such as I remember in use nearly sixty years ago. It is folded in four, and yellow with age, and is, moreover, somewhat soiled, as if often touched with warm but not dirty hands. I cannot be quite positive that it emanated from Wrightson himself; as there is a bare possibility that Wrightson's successor, a man said to have been his nephew, and to have inherited his books, but not, I fear, his native shrewdness and ability – if any other of his better qualities – may have been applied to by the former owner of this paper. But Dawson's – the nephew's – occupation of the office or position of Wise Man was but a short one; and it was so, I was led to suppose, by reason of his utter incompetency to fill the post; and no long time elapsed before he died a wretched death, that of a drunken, miserable, beggarly outcast, 'like a dog by the roadside', as the man who told me about him expressed it. Thus I have no doubt in my own mind about the authorship of this noteworthy manuscript. It reads thus: 'Bleed the Sick animall and Clip in amongst The Blood som hair Cut of the animals mane Tail and 4 Quarters Then put in 3 spoonfuls of

Salt Then have a Sheeps heart stuck with 9 new pins 9 new needles 9 small nails Then rool The heart well in the blood and at 12 at night put The heart on a Good fire of Coals and ash Sticks and as it Burns Read Those Psalms 35—104. 109—56—77 Read Them 3 times over and let all be done by one Oclock make doors and windows fast keep all very Secret and have a Strong faith if this do not answer you must do it twice more at the full and Change of the moon just as you did the first time with fresh Things should This fail you need go to no one else as Thay will nor Can not Cure your Beast.'

This precious formula is written in a firm, bold, unfaltering hand, very plain and legibile. The ocassional misspelling may be noticed, as also that the numeral preceding the words 'new pins' is 59, which, as I have no doubt the number intended was 9 and not 59, I have altered to the former figure. The direction as to the psalms to be read is altogether perplexing. I assume that what is meant is that the psalms so numbered are to be read in the sequence indicated; but it is somewhat difficult to understand the principle upon which the selection was made – assuming, that is, that there was a principle and also a selection.

It only occurs to me further to remark that the use of this formula appears to be very greatly variant from that, resembling it in several particulars, described at a former page. There the intention and the anticipated result were both of the most pronounced anti-witch description. She, the witch, was to be baffled, foiled, defeated, and made to suffer for her misdeeds past. Here the entity even of the witch is not so much as glanced at. The animal, whose illness is supposed, is ill of a lingering disorder; but no imputation as to any person or party's connection with the illness is so much as hinted at, and the formula seems intended to be used with a curative intention only. Just as the witch-wood was understood to be a prophylactic against witches in general, with no personal application, so, it would seem, was it the intention of the present charm to reverse or baffle the malicious practices of some or any witch unknown.

There is yet one topic among the many suggested by the comprehensive term 'Folklore', on which I would willingly add a few remarks. I mean the curious and interesting subject of Bee Notions. They are very various, and some, at least, among them are still very persistent. Such are the ideas that bees bought by the exchange for them of the sterling coin of the realm never thrive with the purchaser; the swarm or hive dwindles and dies out, or perhaps it takes its departure to settle elsewhere than in the place destined for it in the ill-omened trafficking; that a swarm which comes to the bee-keeper adventitiously is lucky, but if claimed by its proper owner, no money must pass for its surrender, or, on the other hand, in consideration of its retention; that if a swarm settles on dead wood, such as a post or rail, or a dead tree or shrub, it surely betokens the imminent death of some member of the household visited; and so forth.

But I think one of the most curious notions is that connected with the manner of dealing with the bees when a death occurs in the household they belong to, and especially when the death in question is that of the master or head of the household. I remember when I was a schoolboy in Essex, my father being then curate of a country parish not far from Colchester, the news came that the rector was dead, which of course implied the consequent removal, after a space of weeks or months, of the curate. But that did not affect me or fix itself on my attention as did the proceedings taken in connection with the bees, of which a large stock belonged to the rectory. I cannot remember who the person acting on behalf of the rectorial family was, or by what authority the said person acted; but I do remember the key of the main door of the house being taken, together with sundry strips of some black material, and a kind of procession organized for a formal visit to the bee-stand. And when it was reached the bearer of the key proceeded to bind a black strip round each hive – this was called 'putting the bees into mourning' – and as each strip was knotted, three taps with the key were given, and each hive severally informed that the master was dead. There was a sort of weird solemnity about the whole proceeding which produced a lasting impression on my young mind.

In after years many things conduced to the retracing and deepening of such impression. I will not enter into details of them, but simply say I was led to notice and collect as well as inquire. While my interest was still fully awake I happened to receive a long letter from the then rector of Sessay, in which, among a variety of other matters, all more or less illustrated by classical quotations, he gave me an account of a recent experience of his when he had been called upon to bury one of his elder parishioners, and had accordingly been 'bidden' to the house where the deceased man was lying, some hours before the 'body was to be lifted' and taken to the churchyard. He told me he had partaken of the accustomed hospitality, and had retired to the garden to smoke his pipe in quiet, and had seated himself accordingly in a sort of arbour or summer-house. Presently his attention was aroused by the passage of a woman, the wife of the eldest son of the deceased man. She was carrying a tray, on which he saw there were piled a variety of eatable and drinkable matters. She went straight to the beehives, and he heard her address the bees themselves. Naming the late owner, she said, 'John G— is dead, and his son is now master. He has sent you something out of every dish and jug on the table, and we hope you will be content to take him as the new master.'

Founded on this were divers inquiries of mine prosecuted in Danby and the Dales district generally, and from my old and helpful friend who was my right hand in most of my barrow-digging undertakings, I ascertained that at no less than four recent 'buryings' he had noticed some observances more or less tallying with those recorded by the Sessay rector. He had seen the bees put into mourning; he had never known the intimation of the death of the late owner and the accession of the successor omitted; and the offering of food and liquor had been, and to some extent was even yet, much more than simply prevalent. And he gave me more than one illustration of the formula employed when the offering was presented. One was, 'So-and-so is dead, and So-and-so is the new master. He has sent you a bite and a sup of whatever there is on the tables, and he hopes you won't be offended.'

I do not think I am acquainted with any part of England in which these bee observances have not obtained, and in the days of my youth I met with them in a still flourishing condition. Of late years they may have not unusually fallen into a condition of decadence, but I have met with some or other among them in different parts of Lincolnshire and in the north in such vigorous existence, within the last ten to fifteen years, that my interest in them has never been permitted to die away. And all the less because at an earlier period still I had been able to connect modern English notions and usages with certain analogues undoubtedly as archaic as they were non-English.

For years ago I had gone through a course of folklore reading, very copious and equally curious, mainly (though not exclusively) Danish and Swedish, in which I had met with quite unanticipated illustrations of a great variety of our Yorkshire superstitions and practices founded upon them; and among others, these bee notions and usages received no little illustration.

It would be tedious to detail the various steps and stages by which I reached my conclusions, and it must suffice to say that after a long course of other reading, mainly Danish, I became acquainted with Hylten Cavallius's *Wärend och Wirdarne*, which not only enabled me to co-ordinate matters derived from various sources, but in many instances gave me lively illustrations proceeding from origins hardly a century old (and some of them much younger still), of many things which had hitherto seemed altogether obscure. It was in this way I was led on to perceive what an important factor, not only in explaining the conceptions involved in the old legends about fights in the old grave-mounds for the possession of the buried sword of a mighty hero, but in clearing up much of the obscurity involving many folklore principles and practices, both ancient and modern, the old animistic theory as propounded by Tylor and others really becomes. Why should we hear as we do of the burial with the dead of articles of food as well as weapons of war and the chase? There is no answer to the question until one remembers that what may be called the animistic entity of the man might be conceived as being in a position to utilize and employ the animistic principle of the food or the weapon. I think there are four if not five constituents, according to Egyptian philosophy, going to make up the complex idea or entity involved in the human being, and although our far-away ancestors may not have realized those subtle definitions and half-metaphysical conceptions, still they were able to realize something as to the fact, and conjecture something as to the particulars, of a state of existence after the mortal life had ceased, and to fashion their own beliefs and practices accordingly.

It is not a little curious as well as interesting to notice the way in which the old popular notion of the ghost or haunting spirit lends itself to the illustration of the matter in hand. When the old lady of the 'Mark's e'en watch', mentioned elsewhere, threatened to 'come again' if her directions touching her burial were not faithfully attended to, or when Jonathan F——'s funeral procession was detained and delayed by reason of the discussion of the church-road notion, and its sequel, it was not merely because the old woman herself, or even the witch-fearing old farmer, had held certain well-defined superstitious notions, but far more because all the survivors principally concerned were themselves, however tacitly and unsuspectingly even, under the influence of exactly analogous feelings and fears. The expressed conviction of the mourners that Jonathan would not 'rest easy in his grave' if borne otherwise than along the church-way – the 'Hellway' of the old mythology – to his last resting-place, meant neither more nor less than what was not only implied in the old wraith-seer's open threat, but acknowledged by her friends. But it is important to observe what a wide and impassable gulf lies between the crude conception of the restless entity breaking through the prison-walls of the grave, or the vindictive coming-again-being (*gengångare* of the Swedish folklore tellings), and that of the 'spirit' of our Christian faith – the one as essentially non-immaterial as the other is impalpable, like 'the baseless fabric of a vision'.

The step from a non-immaterial 'ghost' to an 'animistic principle', a quasi-*umbra* of the dead, who, in such condition of being, might need the corresponding substitutes for his weapons of the old life, for the food and drink by which the old life had been sustained, is not a far or a difficult one, and the conception of the daily-renewed fights and slayings of the Valhalla bit of mythology, with the nightly-renewed banquetings on the as regularly revivified and re-slaughtered boar which furnished the staple *pièce de résistance*, with the equally recurrent bowls of mead and new ale, is one which, when considered in its concomitants and consequences, involves a singularly effective illustration of these singular bee notions and bee usages. The departed bee-owner, in his new condition of being, would require his appropriate arrows, axe-hammer, sword, what not. He would require his appropriate 'victuals and drink'. But much of his drink had depended on the produce of his bees. All the mead that washed down the boarmeat must depend still on the honey they produced. What wonder then that he should be idealized as wanting the busy makers, and, being even more and more actively non-immaterial than the old woman's 'ghost', should be likely to prefer his claim, and make it good moreover by actually 'coming again' and taking possession, if not formally and effectually prevented? The suicide, the executed malefactor, down to not so very far back even in enlightened England, was staked down in his grave, sometimes had his legs or arms strangely hampered with cord or by twisting, simply to prevent his 'coming again', while in parts of Sweden the precautions taken were even of a stranger and (to modern ideas) far more revolting character. Nay, when the corpse was just newly taken from the dwelling-house, scarcely a century ago, the use was to scatter live embers just beyond the threshold, avowedly to bar the road back thither against the *gengångare*; and for the same reason, and with equally little reticence as to the object, the bee-skeps were visited, and a formal intimation conveyed to the occupants that the old owner was departed, and that no summons to wait on and serve him for the future was to be heeded.

In fact, the more one really enters into the story of the folklore still surviving in these dales of ours, until lately so little accessible and so little intruded upon by the people and the opinions of the outside world, the more one finds to suggest how hard has been the struggle between the old paganism and the new Christianity. Survivals of this form or that of the old nature-worship, of the old cults of hero, demigod, traditional divine ancestor, of this or that quaint, dim, blurred, obscure conception of man himself, and his mysterious constitution and attributes, meet one at every turn. The burial of the abortive calf suggests the propitiatory offering to the earth-spirits almost as sensibly or strikingly as the pins cast into the halikeld, or the votive rags tied to the adjoining bush, do that to the spirits of the water, or of the special spring in question. The dead lamb, or other portions or remnants of animal matter, thrown up into the berry-bearing tree have as much to impart to the inquiring observer tracking the once prevalent Odin-cult as has the strangely significative name of the accustomed weather-presage in the clouds which we call 'Noa-ship'. There are places, but not with us in 'thoase deeals', where the name has been biblicized into Noah's Ark; but the old dalesman still abides by the old 'Noa-ship'. And in the homes of our Old Danish fore-elders the equivalent 'Noeskeppet', wherein the final *et* is the postfixed Scandinavian definite article, and the prefix is the easily traced corruption of Odin, tells us an equally plain and (to some) over-true story of the place held a thousand years ago (and who can tell how much earlier or how much later?) by the old northern god of the seas and the weather in the thoughts and notions of the men who went before us in Danby and near.

Truly the ghost notions and the bee notions and bee practices are not hard to comprehend when reviewed under such side-lights as these.

CHAPTER FIVE

Digging Up the Past

I REMEMBER, on one occasion when my father came to pay me a visit here, making arrangements with two or three men to be present the next morning at a large tumulus, grave-mound or houe, known as Herdhowe, and situate at no great distance from the top of the steep hill on the road leading to Guisborough from Whitby, called Gerrick Bank. My object was to show my father what sort of work barrow-digging really was. One of the men I had sent to, a shoemaker by trade, a strong resolute worker, by no means imaginative, but shrewd, hardheaded, 'Yorkshire' through and through in the matter of a bargain, or a deal in horse-flesh, had been a 'pal' of mine in every houe-digging enterprise I had yet undertaken. He it was who, in my maiden essay in that line, when I was creeping carefully, and with cautious scrapings and anxious probings of the soil – for I felt sure we were near a deposit – tiring of my tardy approaches to the centre of expectation, reached forward over my bended back and lowered head, and with his shovel firmly grasped in his nervous hands, made a fell scoop into the thick of the little mound I was delicately shaping; and by his action disclosed the deposit, it is true, but at the expense of shearing off one-third part of a perfectly entire and uninjured cinerary vase. His concern and regret at the consequences of his impatient act were really rather distressing to witness; and his shame at having misunderstood and undervalued my careful and cautious approaches helped to make him one of the most careful as well as most vigilant workers any barrow-digger could possibly be blessed with.

He became also a diligent and effectual helper in a different kind of grubbing or digging, namely, in the search after the 'dialect' or provincial words which it had long since become an object to me to collect and record. No one could exceed him in zeal in this pursuit, and not many in discretion; and it was 'as good as a play' to mark the manner in which, when he remembered or thought he had secured a 'good word' for me, he brought it out; often in the course of a digging, when there was no excitement from an expected or imminent 'find', and almost always set in a very characteristic saying; so that frequently I had the sentence to record, and not just the new word itself only. Such was the case, for instance, with the fine old saying, 'Ill-gotten gear has nae drith (pronounced dreet) wi't'; and again, with a remark touching an old mare of his own, 'She mayn't be ower good at gannin', but she's a maister to eat'. He's still alive, but no longer the man he was. His 'record' as walking postman would be 'bad to beat'; but the unsparing use he has made of his bodily powers has paved the way for worse than mere gradual bodily decay. Still, however, the old interest in our joint diggings remains; and he listened with sympathetic eagerness to the details I gave him a short time ago as to the diggings I had been directing in Skutterskelf Park.

On the morning referred to above, I fell in with this man on his way towards the scene of our intended operations, but at some little distance from it still. He was always ready for a 'bit o' pross', or 'to ho'd talk wiv a body', on any topic of common interest; but this morning he was even eager to talk, for he had something to tell me. He began much as follows: 'Ah nivver could understand what pleasure folks could finnd in fox-hunting; men and hosses and dogs all rinnin' like gaumerils after a nasty, stinking, lahtle beast like yon! But Ah've coomed to see different sin' Ah got to come diggin' wi' you in thoas houes. You'll maybe hardly credit it, but sin Ah gat word fra you yesterday at e'en, Ah framed as if Ah could settle to nowght, only thinking it lang o' t' moorn to come. Well, I gat me to bed middling early, aiming it wad nae be sae lang while moorn, gin Ah could only get a gay good sleep. But bless you, bairn, there wa'n't nae sike a thing as sleeping. Ah tonned (turned) and Ah toommled, and tahms Ah sloommered (dozed) a bit, but wakkened oop again iv a minnit or tweea, while (till) Ah was as wakrife as a backbearaway i' t' glooaming (a bat in the evening dusk). Towards moorn Ah gat me to sleep some mak' (make, way, fashion) or ither, but it wa'n't for lang. Ah began to dream all mak's and manders o' fond things. But all at yance, Ah foonn (found) mysen digging for bare life in this houe we's boon for now, and we coomed on a finnd, a soort of a lile (little) chamber made wi' steean. And in't there was a main big pankin (pancheon, cinerary vase or urn), and it wur near hand full o' bo'nt beeans (burnt bones). Some way – Ah deean't ken how – it gat whemmled ower, and a skull rolled out, nearlings a hail

yan (a whole or entire one). And it looked to be splitten all across the
top; and then it oppened, and out cam' a elephant – and a greeat foul
beast it wur! And Ah warsled (wrestled, struggled) to get out o' t'
rooad, and wiv a skrike and a loup (a shriek and a leap) Ah gat me out
iv the houe, and that minnit Ah wakkened i' truth; and if you'll believe
me, Ah fun (foon, found) myself raxing and striving o' t' fleear
(straining and struggling on the floor) as gin Ah had gaun clean wud
(stark mad). And Ah've considered thae foxhunters 's nae sike feeals as
Ah aimed 'em.'

I do not wonder the man enjoyed those days on the moors among
the grave-hills as he did. We all enjoyed them. I seldom had more than
four men at work at once; they were as many as I could fairly super-
vise and direct. Once or twice I had five or six. But, all save one, who
was casually impressed one day (and whom I never in the course of
years saw smile, or otherwise than grumpy), made almost a gala-day
of a day's digging on the moor with the parson. But the man just noted
seemed to find no more excitement in and preceding the finds than 'a
gowk in finnding its gorpins' (a cuckoo in feeding its fledglings). To be
sure, he relaxed a little over what he called the grub; and no wonder,
for what appetites we all had! It was a veritable picnic, with all the
abandon and enjoyment of a picnic, and with excitement of a very
pleasurable sort superadded. My wife and a friend or two, together
with two or three of my elder lads – boys from ten to fourteen years
old – besides the working men, were the party. And we all of us worked.
The boys had their small spades. I marked out the work, and directed
it; and when there was no near likelihood of a find, took my place
among the working 'navvies'. Two of my men were so well trained
and so trusty that I could, to some considerable extent, leave the super-
vision of the work done by the others to their vigilance. But the moment
any of the recognized signs of an approach to what might prove to be a
deposit were observed, the vicar was warned; and all the work of
localizing the deposit precisely, and of carefully groping and feeling for,
and finally extracting, the precious and probably broken or crushed, as
well as frail, earthen vessel was his exclusive province. And the eager
faces grouped around as the interment began to be defined, especially if
it were a 'pankin' of some dimensions! And the theories that were
broached as to what the contents would prove to be! And then, when it
was finally taken from the place it had occupied for perhaps two thousand years, possibly even for many more than that, the speculations

were renewed, and the value or the interest of the find compared with that or those of some other day.

The measure of success attending these diggings was of course a variable quantity. Speaking generally, however, a 'blank day' was a thing we hardly knew. And this is a remarkable fact. For in the grave-hill researches I have personally conducted – in several cases begun and carried through with my own unassisted labour – with about two exceptions, the mounds we examined had been previously tampered with and opened. Indeed, in every case but one they had been excavated from the apex or summit, and very often terribly mutilated and blundered.

The one exception from the rule of digging down to the centre from above, was in the case of the largest grave-mound in the entire district. The basin-shaped hollow at the summit, betokening the former disturbance, was there; but the height of the hill – originally not less than sixteen feet – had frustrated the efforts of the explorers, and they had opened a drift into the side of the houe. Another, the Herdhowe already named, had been broken into by the menders or makers – or marrers – of the highways for the sake of its stony constituent parts; and in consequence the ugliest-looking gaps and cavities had been left. I believe that this previous work expended on our barrows had been systematic – organized and carried out by treasure-seekers. It is a matter of record that in different parts of the kingdom treasure-hunts of this kind were arranged and effected under the authority of a written permission, duly signed and sealed, from the sheriff of the county. Such documents are still extant, and copies are given in more than one book dealing with the prehistoric antiquities of such and such a district. And although there is no record of any such authority given in this county, so far as I have been able to ascertain, still the idea has been proved to be quite livingly extant down to a very recent period. Once I asked permission from a Moorsholm freeholder, a wealthy rather than merely well-to-do man, to open a very fairly perfect-looking barrow on a part of the moor which had lately been enclosed in virtue of an apportionment which allotted it to him as his own absolute property. My first request was met with a demur, the grounds of which were not stated. The second time it was made on my behalf by a near connection of the owner's, and permission was ultimately conceded; but with the condition attached, that I should make over to him all the silver and gold I might chance to meet with in the course of my excavations. And again, to quote another instance illustrative of the same particular, being one day, with my party of diggers, occupied in the examination of a houe at no great distance from a trackway across the moors leading to Guisborough, one of a small party who were crossing in that direction, after watching us in silence for a few minutes, called out to us, 'What is it you are after there? Are you laiting go'd (seeking gold)?'

But to return to what I was saying, namely, that it was remarkable that, dealing with grave-mounds which all, with scarcely an exception, had been opened before, still we were almost invariably successful. In fact, the success was so great that in the issue my workmen became a little demoralized by it; and, failing the excitement of the accustomed finds, after digging vainly for a while they began to lose spirit, and to work languidly and listlessly until such time as something happened to brighten them up a little. And indeed there was some justification for their excited anticipations; for on one occasion we carried home no less than eight sepulchral vessels of one kind or another; and one of them was found on examination to contain, over and above the usual complement of burnt bones, a very beautiful and finely polished axe-hammer of fine-grained granite. A total of two or three urns from the same barrow was by no means unusual; and while some houes yielded only one interment, or at the most two, others produced three or four. Herdhowe, indeed, yielded in all, counting the distinct evidences of previously rifled and ruined deposits, no less than the extraordinary number of sixteen. There were nine entire urns – including a so-called food-vessel and three small vases such as are usually described under the general but misleading term 'incense-cups' – all added to my collection from that one single source.

And I pause here to notice one particular group of four among the rest of this great find, which was such as to constrain one, entirely against the dictates of his soberer judgement, to hazard a sort of wild-goose guess of what might have been the antecedent reason for their deposit, grouped as they were. For two of the vases in question (small ones all of them) contained each the calcined bones of a child of very tender years; another, the largest of the set, was inverted as well as empty; and the remaining one, besides the bones of an adult of small stature, had in it a perforated bone-pin, or quasi-needle, with the fragments of what had most evidently been a fine cutting instrument of flint, which had flown to pieces in the burning. These four, as I have said, formed a group. The empty – was it a cenotaph? – vessel was a little in the rear.

Advanced a few inches were the two urns with the children's remains; and on a stone, thin and flat and some twenty inches in length, laid over them, stood the fourth vase, containing the needle and cutting-flint.

What theory will my readers devise for themselves touching such a group? For I think the vessels could not have been placed as they were without thought, intention, or object.

Again, another day I went, with only my two eldest boys, lads of twelve and thirteen years of age respectively, and set to work on a tumulus which I knew had been opened before on two different occasions; on the latter, by a party of gentlemen from Whitby, now fifty years ago or more, who left a precise memoir of the results of their investigation, which memoir has since passed into my possession. In this document they speak of the evidences of former opening from above, and of the discovery of the fragments of two large urns which had been found by the previous explorers, broken up (as the manner was) and the sherds thrown carelessly on one side. It was recorded, too, that, though they had carried their trench right through from north to south, they had met with nothing to recompense their labour and pains; and that they were assured there was nothing left beyond the traces of former spoliation as described.

Knowing only too well how utterly unscientific and unthorough all such investigations then were, and having the good reason of considerable experience for thinking that the part of the houe they had left untouched was almost certain to prove the most prolific, I began, after my usual system, on the eastern side of their bootless cutting, at its southern end, working inwards from about a yard within the south-eastern rim of the mound towards the centre. About half-way between the circumference and the centre, and within a few inches only of the eastern edge of the abortive cutting from north to south, my spade suddenly passed through no less than four thicknesses of 'Ancient British' pottery. To say that I was vexed, annoyed, discomfited at such apparent proof of reckless rather than unconsidered working, would be to convey a wrong impression, for I knew I had been working as carefully and as watchfully as usual, and that there had not been any, the slightest, indications of proximity to a deposit hitherto afforded. Besides, the section of material obtained by that one application of the sharp edge of the spade was in itself astounding to an old digger. As described above, my energetic friend with his trenchant shovel shore off at one stroke one-third part of a rather large cinerary vase, but he had only cut through one thickness of the luckless vessel, while I had just cut through four thicknesses! Now we have all seen oranges peeled for the amusement of children by passing a skin-deep incision round the greatest circumference, and proceeding carefully to raise each half of the peel by the use of a spoon or what not, so as to get two cups or bowls (so to speak) each of them comprising half the skin of the orange. Treat two oranges thus, and fitting the one half of the peel of each into the other half, bring the two double cups thus obtained into contact, hollow to hollow, and, more or less roughly, edge to edge. Then press them together so as somewhat to flatten the resulting globe (but without bursting the peel), and pass some sharp cutting instrument transversely through the four thicknesses. The section that will be obtained will be precisely the kind of section just spoken of as effected by my spade, two curvilinear concave edges opposed to two other concave curvilinear edges precisely like. I need not say that curiosity was stirred, or that close and careful investigation was prompted. With every possible care and delicacy a space of more than two feet square was laid bare, and then the mystery stood revealed, – at least a certain measure of it did, not quite all. Over the whole area exposed, portions of a large urn were dispersed, and with them the calcined bones which it had once contained. In that particular part cut through by the spade the chief part of the said vase had been laid (or thrown), one concave piece within the other, and two such composite pieces opposed to other two like, just as with our supposed orange peel. In the very middle of this medley of burnt human bone and sherds of the old imperfectly baked vessel stood a small delicately moulded and decorated vase of the type usually called 'incense-cups', with its own proper deposit of incinerated remains and accompanying flints. I described it as follows in the *Gentleman's Magazine* at the time: 'One inch in height and under one inch and a half in greatest diameter, of red ware, and scored with lines crossing one another diagonally, but so as to leave a space of three-eighths of an inch all round, nearest to the bottom, untouched. It was placed mouth upwards, in the centre between four flints laid east, north, south, and west, and comprising a very flat leaf-shaped, arrow-point, another of the same description, but thicker, a thumb-flint or scraper, and some other implement; but all of them coarsely or rudely fashioned and chipped – that is, as compared with many others found by the writer.

These were both, and quite obviously, what are called 'secondary deposits . The houe had not been originally built or piled over them.

They were later – and who shall say how much later? – than the mound itself as originally fashioned. Perhaps even the original mound had been added to or enlarged on purpose to qualify it for receiving these later interments, each in its own proper sequence. For again it is perfectly obvious that there were two insertions in succession – the disturbed or descrated one, and that which had led to or caused the disturbance or desecration. For the present I leave the idea suggested by the alternative terms employed for a little consideration.

There is a good deal of speculation involved in the alternative terms made use of at the close of the last section. Was what had been observed the result of disturbance, or was it accidental only? Or had it been desecration, intended, systematic, effectual? I remember well what I felt rather than thought as I opened out that questionable deposit. For the time being I entertained no doubt of the intention and the object, namely, that desecration, reckless and purposed interference with the remains of one departed, was the end sought. I had been doubtful in divers other cases. I had thought the interference with, or the displacement of, a previous burial which had come under my notice in earlier explorations might be best and most easily explained as accidental and unintended. Thus there had been an examination of a large houe on the Skelton Moors, sixty-three feet in diameter, in which, at a point twenty feet south of the centre, I had found an inserted cairn, or conical pile of stones, of very considerable size for only an 'insertion', and which covered incontestable evidences of disturbance of a previous burial, if not of more than one. The pile had flat stones laid slopingly round and over it. They were of considerable size, and when they were removed they left the appearances of hollow spaces within, which led one to expect the speedy discovery of deposits. Half an hour spent in careful work disclosed the site of the main deposit intended to be protected or signalized by the cairn, and near it a small incense cup of red clay inverted and quite without ornament. 'There were many stones of the pile still to be removed, several of them below the exact place where the cup had just been found; and at a level lower by at least a foot, numerous fragments of another red urn, accompanied by portions of calcined bone, which had assumed a clay colour, and were much decomposed as well as scattered about, were met with, and under such circumstances that there could be no reasonable doubt that they belonged to a deposit anterior in point of date to that found just before, and disturbed in the process of excavating the bed on which the cairn enclosing that had been raised. This urn was completely disintegrated, and its various mouldering portions found in divers different parts of an area of fifteen or eighteen inches square.' And my contemporaneous commentary on all this was as follows: 'This barrow was a most interesting one, and certainly wonderfully illustrative of the custom of burying continuously in a barrow already formed. No less than nine interments, clearly, and ten urns were discovered; besides which, the distinct chronological connection of three of them is clearly indicated. First, the tumulus was raised over the remains of some one of note or importance. Then, and one cannot even guess how long afterwards, a secondary deposit was made on the southern flank. Then again, and doubtless after many years, a third internment was made on the very site of this last mentioned, causing the entire demolition of its accompanying urn and the dispertion of the incinerated remains enclosed.' It is clear, then, that I did not then think – it is now twenty-six years ago – of anything but a chance or accidental disturbance of the previous burial. Years and years in that dim far-away past had come and gone, and the precise locality of this secondary interment had been forgotten, or lost sight of. That was what was in my mind when fresh from the contemplation of the circumstances. But how about this other, where the entire previous deposit had been deliberately spread, or rather scattered about, in order to make room for, and, as it were, wait in degraded subjection upon, the latter deposit of the bones of a deceased superior – and superior, it might be, in virtue of a stronger arm, or of a greater and overwhelming force?

In truth there were many things in the interior of these old-world burying-places to set the thoughtful man thinking and the speculative man imagining, guessing, reconstructing. No two of those of the larger size were built of the same material, or planned on precisely the same principle. In one I found a circular platform of symmetrically piled stone. It was twenty feet in diameter, nearly six feet in vertical depth, with a cist neatly constructed in the centre, and the entire level surface of it covered, six inches deep, with the whitest, snowiest sand. It was years upon years – twenty-four or twenty-five, I should say – before I ascertained where that sand could have been procured from. I knew of its existence, but not in anything like sufficient purity to supply a tithe of what I saw bestrewing that platform. And the place at which, as I at last ascertained, it could have been obtained in the requisite whiteness and quantity, was at least seven miles distant in a linear direction!

Not perhaps that that would make any difference to those devoted builders. For, in one large and still symmetrical houe at the foot of Freeburgh Hill – the very grave-mound in which I obtained the conditional permission to dig recorded above – I found, on the natural surface, and concentric with the mound itself, a cairn or conical pile of stones, many of them as heavy as, putting forth all my strength, I could lift, the base of which was sixteen feet in diameter and the height six. And every one of those stones was so marked in character that I had no more uncertainty about the place of their origin than I had about the dwelling-places of the men who were working with me or merely looking on in wondering curiosity.

Everybody has heard of the 'whinstone dike' that runs transversely across Cleveland, entering the district no great way from Yarm and running a south-easterly course of nearly thirty-five miles, only slightly deflected from a perfectly direct line. It was this whinstone or basaltic dike which had furnished every individual block in the whole of that very considerable cairn; and the nearest point at which it could have been obtained in the quantities employed was at least three miles and a half away, and across the untracked moor, with swamp and morass to cross and recross on the route.

In the case too of another grave-hill nearer home, the great constituent mass thereof consisted of clean water-worn pebbles and nodules of half a dozen different varieties of stone, such as could have been derived only from the bed of a beck running its course to the sea through a moor-valley some two miles and a half distant.

As a rule I should say that the constituent materials of all the largest houes – and some of them are very large, one being ninety-five feet in diameter at the base and even still thirteen feet in height – were brought from a distance. There are no signs of excavation, or even of removal of the former surface, anywhere in their vicinity; I have ascertained that by direct personal examination. I am inclined to think too that the work was done not only very carefully but very systematically, whether merely for the due preservation of symmetry, or (it might be) under the direction of some chief, or the personal oversight and engineering of some skin-clad 'clerk of the works', with curiously tattooed body and limbs.

For, in divers different hills, when I had succeeded – often at the cost of some sensible amount of personal labour – in obtaining a good clean section of the interior of a grave-hill, I have observed a significant regularity of stratification, always following the outline of the mound, as that outline must have been in the early days of its being. And this stratification was such in its character as to show conclusively that the material was not only derived from diverse localities, involving different colours and various qualities, but also deposited, when obtained and brought to the site of its destined application, with the steady regularity which characterizes systematized and methodical as well as graduated, accretion. By way of illustration of what I mean: One often sees a railway embankment in process of construction. Coup-cart after coup-cart is tipped at the edge of the slowly growing and lengthening mound, and the contents of each go streaming down the sloping face in inter-mingling and irremediable confusion. There is no such thing as stratification there, even though sand and gravel, clay and peat, loam and vegetable soil are all being brought up in unfailing supply. In the houes, on the other hand, there is often well-defined stratification. Not that there was not an unfailing supply also in those days of houe-build-ing, as long as the demand lasted at least; but what was brought was carefully strown and neatly evened over the whole surface of the rising mound.

But to turn to quite another topic, and matter also for some little attentive consideration. I hardly think that on these wide and wild moors in this division of the district of Cleveland the custom as to the actual placing of what remained of the body after cremation – for no one actual instance of inhumation simple has so far been met with – varies at all, except in the rarest instances. The incinerated remains were simply laid on the natural surface, whether with the protection or accompaniment of an urn or without, and then covered over with earth, and whether with or without the protection of some sort of rough or rude stone-work. Once, and once only, have I found a plat-form of stones, in a cist wrought in which the body had been placed; and once, and once only, a platform of earth on which the accom-panying urn had been placed; and once, and once only, a shallow excavation or grave, which had been the receptacle of the original deposit – speaking, of course, of the 'original deposit' only.

As to the 'secondary burials', they seem to have been made, at least occasionally, in excavations hollowed out in the side of an existing grave-mound. Perhaps, even, that was the rule. But there can be no doubt that in many cases these secondary interments led on not only to very considerable additions to the existing grave-hill, but to additions of such magnitude as entirely to remodel the grave-mound dealt with. Thus, in one instance – that of the mound, about his adventures in which my faithful helper dreamed his dream, and in which I ascertained that, from first to last, no less than sixteen cinerary vases had been deposited – what I had no doubt had been the original work of the hill, namely, a shallow pit of sixteen feet in length by something less in width, filled in and piled over with a cairn of stones, had been thrown some eight feet out of the centre by subsequent additions, chiefly on the southern and eastern flanks.

But whatever the alteration on the original pile, or the deviation from the original ground-plan, there was no departure from the rule of symmetry. Wherever enough of the mound stands as when it was left as finished by its builders, to guide one's conclusions, the base is regularly circular, and the sides slope up with the graceful lines of the accurately-shaped cone. And not unseldom there are as evident signs of careful and diligent pains expended over the exterior as in the general and consistent construction of the whole great mass of the barrow. In many instances the more considerable among these remnants of antiquity are girt in at the base with large containing stones, laid slopingly, so as not to interfere with the even outline of the sloping sides. Sometimes even an exterior ring of encircling stones, sunk deeply enough into the earth to have remained firm fixtures during the long wear and tear of five-and-twenty or thirty centuries, is found.

Truly these men of the past, whoever they were, and whatever they were, and whencesoever they came, wrought great and abiding memorials, leaving traces behind them that but few are disposed to notice without a sort of sneer for those who care for them, but which yet are more full of material for thought than five-sixths of the books which cumber the modern bookstall.

I go into a graveyard of the day that now is – into this quiet, remote, reposeful one around my own parish church, if you will – and I see there headstones by the hundred, all of them, with the exception of a scant half-dozen, tasteless, ill-shapen, ugly, meaningless, hopeless, wretched erections; with an occasional equally unprepossessing monument – 'thruff', as it is termed here, – and one or two plain slabs lying flush with the turf. If I examine them with some care and attention to date, and so forth, I find two or three that record the burial of persons who were still living in the latter part of the seventeenth century. If I

want anything of the sepulchral 'in memoriam' type, I have to look in
the walls of the church-yard, or in the lintel of the door out of the basement of the tower (which does duty as the porch to the right modern
church of to-day), and there I can see bits of floriated crosses on portions of the original coffin-covers, or perhaps a stray entire one, just
saved from utter demolition because they admitted of being employed
in the mason-work of the alteration! These once covered the remains
of men of position in the parish, perhaps of knightly rank; but we know
no more of them than we do of the builders of the grave-mounds on
the moors. And those great imposing grave-mounds will survive, as
durable as ever, if left only to the hand of time, when the crosses on
those grave-slabs shall have mouldered away ages before; while, as to
the headstones which disfigure as well as crowd the churchyard, where-
on the pagan 'urn' contends for supremacy as an emblem – of what? –
with the Christian cross, they are already put to self-invited shame by
the enduringness of the piles which were raised to cover the urns they
feebly mimic, the urns that enclosed the still enduring ashes of those
who had no cross to cling to!

One thing else. I am told that it is a shameful thing, an abuse, to vio-
late the graves of the dead, to disinter the remains of those committed
to their 'last resting-place', as is done in barrow-digging. Many a
philippic of that sort I have had to listen to, and to read. I suppose that
is a part of the rampant cant of the day. I am sure I have seen more
desecration of churchyards, more interference of the most shameful
and shameless kind with 'the last resting-places of the dead', in one
case of a 'restoration' of an old parish church, than has been occasioned
by all the excavations of all the barrow-diggers united! I have actually
seen cartload after cartload of mingled earth and human remains – the
latter now and then predominating – taken out of the churchyard of one
watering-place in the North of England (the church of which was undergoing restoration), and carelessly thrown down on the cliff!

And yet further, let us not forget that there was something to be
gained, some knowledge to be acquired, in and by and through every
instance of careful and observant barrow-digging properly carried out.
The feeling that in and through our work we were trying – and not
altogether unsuccessfully – to decipher a partly obliterated page of
history, has been sometimes so strong in my own individual case, that
it hardly seemed a mere stretch of erratic imagination to try and form a
mind-picture of the old dwellers among these wastes, whose abiding

memorials I was dealing with. I have long ceased to look upon the groups of pits which have been christened 'British villages' as connected even in the remotest degree, with our 'Ancient British' predecessors. But it was otherwise indeed with the old and by no means – at least when properly questioned – uncommunicative grave-mounds of the wild moors.

Although the last thing I said was that the connection of the groups of pits, so-called 'British villages', with our ancient British predecessors was a matter I had long ceased to look upon as probable or indeed reasonable, still I hardly propose to enter into a consideration of the reasons which have led me into such an instance of unbelief as that is, just at present. I can only say now that I believe the object with which they were excavated, and the epoch of the excavation, have to be inquired for in a widely different direction from any indicated by the name they are credited with and made to bear.

But although it may be, and is, idle to look for any traces of habitation amidst these misnamed, or rather misdescribed pits, and especially of such a date, or, perhaps, anywhere in this district, it is not idle to look for traces of occupation – occupation as distinct from habitation. They are to be seen, and seen distinctly, in many different directions. But they are mostly of one character, and the indications they afford are nearly all of the same general nature and bearing.

It is true, I am told of 'camps' and 'British strengths', and even 'castles'; and I regret to see the authority of the Ordnance Survey pledged to such statements. For while I know that many of them are altogether imaginary, and others utterly suspicious, in very few cases are the accepted designations or allegations to be fully depended upon.

But it is otherwise with the 'dikes', 'intrenchments', 'trenches', etc., many of which are marked, and others left unnamed, if not unnoticed, in the Ordnance sheets, and undescribed or misdescribed by local writers. They all have a legend to be read, if only there be one sufficiently versed in such lore to decipher it. Not that the task is easy, or the interpretation self-suggesting and unmistakable. I take, for instance the dikes or intrenchments which cross the ridges of moorland, between which lie our dales of Glaisdale, Fryup Dale (Great and Little), Danby Dale, Westerdale, etc. None of these have less than two lines of defence crossing them, and some of them have three, and even four, or at least have had; for the clean stone of which more than one of them were constructed had, since the times of enclosure, and especially of drainage, came in, proved a strong attraction to the farming freeholders to plunder, and eventually entirely destroy them by total removal of their material.

Moreover, all these dikes seem to have one general feature in common, and to indicate one special intention. As defensive works at all, they are defensive against attack delivered from the south, and in no other direction whatever. Wherever the works are left sufficiently undamaged by time or depredation to admit of adequate examination, that is the direct testimony of them. There is one, for instance – one out of two, moreover – across what is named the Castleton Ridge in the one-inch Ordnance map, and therein designated the 'High stone-dike', of which a small section is yet so far intact as to permit it to be definitely asserted that the front of it (looking south) has been faced with stone, and had a deep ditch before it. Besides, as it would appear from what is left still standing, stone posts have been set thickly along the crest of it, of nearly four feet in height above the surface, and yet almost flush with the aforesaid stone-faced front.

Granted what is thus premised, of course the question arises, Against what attacks, directed from the south, against what assailants, were these defences designed and erected? Were they meant for bulwarks against the onset of the men of one tribe or tribelet, dwelling in the Farndale, Rosedale, Wheeldale valleys, or, in other words, the people of the valleys south of the watershed furnished by the line of the Cleveland Hills, delivered upon the inhabitants of the general district lying north of the said ridge line; or had they some totally distinct object and end from any of such a merely local and arbitrary supposition?

For my own part, after walking over and along these ancient earthworks, some of them so elaborate, and all evidently forming a part of a single and individual system, extending several miles in their dale-interrupted course from east to west, I have become less and less able to entertain the view that the tribes on the south – supposing that phraseology can be looked upon as sufficiently admissible, if not accurate – were likely to live in a state of chronic warfare with the tribes of the north. Indeed, I do not in the least believe in such distinction of tribes so sharply defined. I do not think it even possible that there should have been a hard-and-fast line of demarcation between two sets of people of the same general family who could have differed, and did differ only – so far as our means of testing the matter go – in living a few miles north, or a few miles south, of a certain geological 'axis'.

But if not war between contiguous tribes or tribelets, warfare between what two sets of combatants could have led up to and occasioned the erection of the earthworks in question?

In order to try and answer this question to my own more or less complete satisfaction, I have said to myself: 'If General Pitt Rivers's researches and investigations touching the Danes Dyke, the Argam Lines, the Scamridge Dykes, go for anything – and surely the patient, systematic, long-continued inquiries of a military engineer, with all the special advantages in and by that designation implied, ought to go for something – then surely the results and deductions he had arrived at in an investigation which more than probably presents many points of analogy with the question we have ourselves propounded, not only ought not to be overlooked by us, but most likely will be found to be by no means without suggestiveness.'

His conclusions seemed to be something of this nature: That the Danes Dyke was a defensive work thrown up, not by the denizens of the land, but by an invading force, coming by sea necessarily; that it, the said dyke, consituted a base for their invasive operations, and that having acquired mastery over a given area in their front, they pushed still farther forward, protecting their advance by another work, on the same principle, namely, the Argam Lines; and that, pursuing the same tactics, they advanced farther into the interior from thence, protecting both their front and their flanks by other earthworks, which still remain in more or less of their being to attest alike the strategy and the skill with which the invasive progress was devised and conducted.

And then next came the question, 'Who' – or, if that could not be answered – 'What, of what age and period, or quality, were these said invaders?'

An answer of some sort, perhaps as satisfactory as, under the circumstances, could have been anticipated, was obtained by the process of cutting through the so-called Danes Dyke in divers places, with the view of ascertaining, if possible, if any, and if so what, indications as to the people who really constructed those huge works might possibly be found buried in those old banks of earth and stones. And one section in particular – nearly all of them affording something or other in the shape of indication – one section in particular might almost be termed communicative from the nature and amount of the information it conveyed. For it disclosed the fact that the men who threw up the fortification not only used flint implements, but made them, and, moreover, made them on the spot.

We find flint chippings, flint flakes, flint implements even (of the commoner sort), in the graves in our churchyards; a fact which just proves that the users and makers of flint objects had once lived in the district. We find scrapers, flakes, drills, knives, arrow-points, all of flint, in and about the barrows so continually and systematically, that we know they were scattered or deposited (as the case might be) of set purpose, by those who raised the barrows as well as used the flint. And I have myself found three places on these moors where the chippings, *spiculae*, remnants of flint of divers characters, as plainly showed that flint implements and weapons had been manufactured there, as the matters commonly lying about a blacksmith's shop show the vicinity (past or present) of the forge. And just such indications of the manufacture of flint were found in the very thick of the dike, not scattered about as in our grave-mounds, and so much more sparingly in our church-yards, but as thickly spread as you find the shavings and scraps and odds and ends of wood below the joiner's bench. The inference was obvious. While the works, misnamed the Danes Dyke, were yet in progress, while they lacked still some feet of the intended or ultimate height and massiveness, some among the host of the builders were plying their vocation as makers and fashioners of those indispensable flint weapons and implements. There lay the little piles and accumulations of the chips and refuse material, ready to be covered up and preserved by the next course in the building of the bulwark, and for discovery and cross-questioning and interpretation by the modern military engineer.

Yes, the devisers and builders of those massive and skilfully projected lines of defence were makers and users of flint weapons and flint implements; and yet that is not a fact inconsistent with a knowledge, on their part, and possession of instruments and weapons of metal. On the contrary, all that we know – and it is no little nowadays, thanks to the scientific, accurate, and painstaking researches and records of such men as Greenwell, Pitt Rivers, Rolleston, and others of the same school – of the men who raised the round barrows that stud the high grounds of our country, tends to the assurance that they were possessors and users of bronze for their tools and weapons, as well as fabricators and employers of the more primitive flint. What then is to hinder the inference that the Danes Dyke invaders, wielders of bronze weapons as well as users of flint-headed arrows and javelins, prevailed over the simply stone-weaponed denizens of the land of which they had arrived as the invaders; that, as prevailing, they became occupiers; and that, as occupiers, they left those intelligible, if not communicative, memorials of themselves which have been so abundantly met with in the grave-mounds and earthworks of the district?

But, suppose all this admitted as regards the origin and purpose of the works we know under the name of the 'Danes Dyke', the 'Argam Lines', and the 'Scamridge Trenches', can we for a moment maintain the theory that the only landing-place available to or utilized by such invaders was just that particular point on the Yorkshire coast which afforded ready access to the headland which was made defensible by the casting up of these great lines of defence? The merest consideration of the circumstances in their general significance – to say nothing of the knowledge derivable from what is known of later invasions made from the same side of the North Sea – leads on inevitably to the conclusion, not so much that there may have been, as that there must have been, divers and sundry raids from over the sea upon the old stone-weaponed inhabitants of the land, made at different times and at various places. And it is much more than merely possible that these lines of defence, and of defence, moreover, against possible or menaced attack from the south, to which attention was drawn a little above, may all admit of the same kind of explanation as Danes Dyke near Flamborough Head, and its more inland accessories.

And if this be so, one of the first inquiries to be made must of necessity be, 'Where should the base to correspond with the base identified in the Danes Dyke be looked for in this more northerly part of the country? Can any suggestion of even a possible similar site be made?' And I think the answer may not be far to seek.

The very remarkable fortification at Eston Nab, which has given occasion for so many wild guesses and unreasonable hypotheses, remains as yet totally unexplained and totally unappropriated, and might well challenge, at the hands of come competent local antiquary, or some scientific Society in the district, some such careful and scienti-fically conducted inquiry as that which has resulted in the happy identification of the real origin and purpose of the strong ancient lines near Flamborough, and across the inland route from thence.

At least this much is certain, that while the Ordnance Survey amply suffices, even where the possibilities of personal examination do not exist, to demonstrate that certain lines of communication between the Cleveland seaboard and the interior are cut across and blocked by carefully, often elaborately, devised intrenchments, the only conclusion admissible is that, at the times indicated by the construction of the said lines, the only route or routes available for a body of men to move along on such an expedition were just these lines of way so blocked. For the merest and most superficial examination of the entire Dales district is sufficient to show that even in the earlier historic period, all that was not moorland was a series of swampy marshes, intergrown rather than overgrown with wood and forest. And one has but just to dip into such a book as Green's *Making of England* in order to become aware of what the barriers were that were presented to hinder or forbid the further advance of better equipped as well as better armed invaders of many centuries later, by marsh and swamp, forest and wood, and other such natural defences.

But while firmly believing that all the works which have been referred to afford indications, not of small intertribal scuffles or skirmishes, but of systematic military advances from the seaboard into the interior, and that they can only belong to the same date, and be attributed to the same constructors as the numerous and most instructive grave-mounds of the district (so many of which have been made to yield up their hidden testimony), I still find myself totally unable to agree with those who have had no difficulty in discovering any number of 'British villages' almost at command. But this is a subject which deserves to begin a new section.

CHAPTER SIX

Ancient Britain

I SUPPOSE there must be something very attractive in the British Village theory akin to the delight of castle-building or the weaving of Alnaschar's famous dreams. I have seen pilgrimage after pilgrimage paid to the alleged British Village on the Danby low moors. People used to come up in carriage loads from Whitby, to see it; and now, in the time of trains, the number of votaries, notwithstanding the distance from the station and the difficulty of the walk, does not fall off; and they look at the holes in the ground, and, I suppose, they go away happy. I remember once on a time taking a learned Greek professor, afterwards Master of his college, to see the said 'settlement', warning him first that walking through the ling from the Beacon – as far as which point I had driven him in my pony-trap – and back again, might prove no joke to his professorial legs. As we went down the slope from the hill bearing the said Beacon he smiled superior to the idea of a tramp through the ling proving fatiguing. He smiled also on scanning the instructive line of holes in the soil, with tufts of rushes growing in them. But he smiled no longer when we took the slope the other way on, and had to make our way through ling mid-thigh high. But he smiled again, and benignantly too, when, some three hours later, he was seated at my dinner-table, and felt himself refreshing and in a fair way of reaching the perfect tense of the operation; but this time it was his own simplicity in undertaking such an expedition for such a questionable object that he smiled at. And veritably the craze is a funny one.

Because it is nothing but a craze, and a most manifest craze, on the face of it, in the great majority of instances; and it is hard to deal with the way in which the theory is delivered in any other sense. The preposterous rubbish, for instance, written by Ord in his *History of Cleveland*, touching what he calls 'British habitations', might be enough, one would think, to show any thinking person the unstable basis on which the British village theory is made to rest: 'Large oval or circular pits, eight to twelve feet deep, and sixty to eighty and a hundred yards (!) in circumference', and 'many hundreds in number' – truly any one who can swallow that as the first item in a description of the aggregated dwellings of the scattered and scanty population of half a dozen, perhaps a score centuries before Caesar, with whom bronze implements must have been about as common and as procurable as silver dinner-plates and dishes among our village populations now, will have no occasion to 'strain at' any 'camel' that is likely to follow. Probably, if Mr. Ord had been set to work with the best and sharpest wood-axe and saw procurable for love or money, to roof over a pit – not thirty yards in diameter, or even twenty, but a modest excavation – of half a dozen yards wide, with poles cut from the forest, and rushes from the marsh, or ling from the moor, and then to maintain his spouse and his progeny with the precarious supplies derivable from hunting, and the hardly less doubtful produce of his herds, flocks, or agricultural toil, he might have thought twice before proposing to domicile some hundreds – not of persons, but – of families in such dwellings and on such sites as his absurdly 'tall talk' asserts rather than assumes.

For my own part, I am exceedingly doubtful whether, in even one single instance of all the British villages or settlements alleged, the claim for such consideration can be shown to have any reasonable, and much more any satisfactory, ground to rest upon. There is no extant record of any really careful and conclusive examination of any one of the pits by competent, qualified, and intelligent investigators. There is no satisfactory proof adduced in any of the accounts or so-called records of such attempts that the true and actual bottom of the excavation operated upon had really been reached, or, indeed, nearly approached.

I remember a great archaeological authority telling me one day of the way in which he had had shown to him a series of pits, with a striking local name, some of which had been 'opened' under the auspices of a local Scientific and Literary society; and how he was assured that the bottom had been reached in this pit and in that; and with all the particulars or accompaniments of charcoal, stones affected by fire, etc. etc.; and how, in his inexcusable (though latent) incredulity he had craved, and not without some persistence obtained, his desire for further excavation in one of the already (perfectly!) explored cavities. Two feet below the previously 'ascertained' bottom unquestionable proofs were obtained that, as old Edie Ochiltree expressed it on a somewhat similar occasion, 'the ground had been travelled before', and the assembled science and literature began to feel surprised, and look perplexed. To make a long story short, my archaeological friend afterwards instituted investigation on his own accouunt; and the upshot was that he had to go down, with patient, persevering excavation, to the depth of thirty-three feet before he reached the real bottom of the pit, which had been regarded as fully and satisfactorily explored by the local philosophers.

But even that was but a beginning of what knowledge and experience, or, in one word, science, enabled the new investigator to achieve, in the way of ascertained knowledge of facts, as regards the great group of hitherto mysterious pits he was working among. He discovered that all the pits, scattered about in rude quincunx form, just like the great majority of our so-called British villages, communicated with one another by a series of low-roofed galleries at the real level of the ascertained bottom. He discovered the tools with which the ancient excavators had worked, and the object for which they had worked. For just where the sinking ceased there had been a six-inch layer or vein of flint, such as to be available for manufacture of flint implements and weapons. This had been won, not only over the area of the actual bottom of the shaft, but as far under the encircling sides of it as it was safe to excavate; and then the sinking of another shaft from the surface had been commenced, and the same process again pursued at its bottom as in the previous one, so as to lead on necessarily to what has been mentioned above as a galleried system of communication of shaft with shaft.

Now, rejecting altogether Mr. Ord's 'hundreds of habitations of from sixty to eighty and a hundred yards in circumference', I do not think any one pit in all the hundreds of pits which are ticketed with the name of British village, has ever been subjected to such an examination as were these old flint-mines in Norfolk by Canon Greenwell. Indeed, I do not think that, if there had been a whole Committee of such inquirers and historians as Ord so abundantly proves himself to have been, the merest notion of what to look for, or how to look for it, would have so much as risen in the brain of any one of them. They would have looked for a charcoal of a foregone conclusion, and found it; they would have looked for a preconceived bottom, and found it. But as to ascertaining, actually ascertaining beyond the possibility of a dispute or doubt, that it really was the veritable bottom, or, being the bottom, why it was so, and how far all round the circumference it extended, or did not extend, – why, neither the mode of examination required, nor yet the grounds on which it was required, would so much as have presented themselves to their imaginations. They would simply have looked for a preconceived bottom to a preconceived habitation, they would have dubbed the search with the grand names of examination and investigation, but they would have ended as they began, with their own preconceived notions – nothing else.

But what might not have been the results of a systematic and scientific investigation, on the other hand, properly and exhaustively carried on by competent and trustworthy inquirers? It would at least have been ascertained what the noteworthy groups of pits were not, even if nothing very definite in the way of actually deciding their real character had been met with. But my own conviction is that the origin and object of the pits grouped together as they are would, in the majority of cases, if not in all, have been actually and fully ascertained; and that it would have proved identical with the conclusion which is suggested by observation of the geological character of the vicinities wherein they are found, illustrated by a little experimental as well as local knowledge.

What I mean by 'the geological character of the vicinity' will be better shadowed forth, perhaps, if I say that I believe that wherever a group of the pits in question in eastern Cleveland and the vicinity of Whitby Strand is met with, a fairly accurate geological map shows also the presence, at or near the surface, of some seam or other of ironstone; and what I think and mean by 'local and experimental knowledge and observation' will be best illustrated by the following relation. It was an object with me some six or seven years ago to collect whatever local information I could, bearing in any way on the somewhat obtrusive fact that, at a long-ago time, the reduction, although not the actual smelting, of iron had gone on largely in this immediate district. Quite forty years ago I had become aware from a variety of historical sources, that iron had been worked in various parts of this and the adjoining North Riding divisions; and even before that, I had noted the fact that the traces of the said working still existed in nearly a score of different places, almost all situate in my own parish and in what once had been a part of it, and all as striking as they were numerous.

What I especially refer to were the hills or mounds, many of them of very considerable, and some of them of very large dimensions, composed of nothing else than the slag which had resulted from the obviously very incomplete reduction of the iron ore. These hills had the common name of 'cinder-hills'. But all tradition, all trace indeed, of any survival of recollection as to the time when, or the way in which, they had been accumulated had ceased to be, and to all, appearance had so ceased for a long time past. Still they were unmistakable indications of what once, in the far-away past, had certainly been.

As inquiry went on, and I slowly succeeded in gathering together a series of facts of one kind or another, all bearing upon the subject of investigation, I became aware that in one part of the parish, and within the memory of living men, structural remains had existed, the former object of which my informant could not explain, but which, from his description of them, I could only infer had been built and used in the production of the iron the manufacture of which had led to the accretion of those huge mounds of slag. The size, shape, mode of construction of these remains all tallied with what I had got to know about the simplest sort of furnaces used in the early epochs of the process of reducing iron-ore. And what was almost more, there lay in the close vicinity a cinder-hill, a large mound, in fact, which had been much drawn upon by the road-makers of no very distant date in order to be employed in the making and mending of the cross-roads in the near neighbourhood of the Fairy Cross Plains already more than once mentioned above.

Naturally, having satisfied myself that the ancient furnace or rather group of furnaces was here in juxtaposition with the slag which had resulted from their operation the next question was, 'Where did the ironstone which it was apparent had been abundantly used actually come from?'

No one knew. No one could even hazard a guess.

Eventually, however, I referred the question to one of the gentlemen employed on the Ordnance Geological Survey, who had been occupied in that part of the district, and with whom I had frequently spoken on such topics. His reply was remarkable, for it was to this effect: 'You have asked me a question which is, in a sort, a little puzzling; for all I can say in answer is that the ironstone available for a furnace in the position indicated by you ought to show itself at this point and at that point,' indicating two recognizable places on the six-inch map, one of them only separated by the modern highway from the site of the furnace and slag-heap which were the subjects of my inquiry; 'but,' he continued, 'it certainly does not show itself at either of these two points.'

This was, as I said, remarkable. The geological surveyor knew exactly where to look for the mineral; only the mineral was not there. Only a day or two later a purely fortuitous circumstance enabled me to explain its absence. And this circumstance befell as follows.

I wished to test the accuracy of my recollection of what had been told me about these assumed furnaces by the man who, as a boy, had been, as he had told me, in the habit of playing 'hide-and-seek' in them. The narrative, as he proceeded to give it, ran almost *verbatim* as my memoranda recorded it. But as he concluded, he added this: 'You remember, sir, my old father-in-law held the farm on which this particular spot is, for some little time after you first came into this country?' Of course I remembered the circumstance and poor old Jonathan equally well. In fact, the spell or charm described on another page was his, and his were the anti-witch proceedings also noticed above. 'Well,' continued my interlocutor, 'when he died, all his papers and suchlike came into my possession; and among the rest there was a farm-plan of the holding he occupied, and in it every field marked with its own name; and among them, of course, the field just across the road that runs past these old furnaces and the cinder-hill: and the name it was called by was "Mine-pit Field." '

Here was an explanation indeed. No wonder my geological friend could not find the ironstone where it ought to have been, seeing it had all been mined away from the immediate vicinity in the manner indicated by the name of the field in question; that is to say, by a series of pits or shallow shafts worked down to the level of the seam, so as to enable the sinkers to win all the ore at the bottom of each shaft, and as much besides as they could reach all round, by the process of undermining the walls of the circular shaft as far as it was safe to do so – a system thoroughly well known in different parts of the kingdom under the name of the 'Bell-pit system'.

But my purpose in mentioning this incident is not merely to illustrate the connection of furnace, slag-heap, and ironstone seam, but is of quite another nature. I had known that field for near forty years, walked over it, shot over it, speculated even from how great a distance the ironstone which had been reduced just across the road had been brought for the purpose. But there was nothing in or about the field to indicate the former existence of mines or pits, or depressions even, anywhere near. No one remembered anything of the kind. No tradition, however dim, existed. And yet the pits had been there. The old field-name left no doubt of that.

But most likely, if they had remained till our own day we should have had a 'British village' the more in the parish.

As a matter of fact, one day when I was prosecuting my inquiries touching the slag-heaps or cinder-hills in Glaisdale, which, in a certain sense, I knew where to look for, because I knew more or less about the limits within which they had been formed during the thirteenth and two following centuries by the canons of Guisborough – these holy men having been empowered by certain definite grants from the great lords of the district, namely, the De Brus barons, to dig mines, build furnaces, and make charcoal to reduce the iron with – I hunted up a certain old friend of mine, whom I had long known as one of the shrewdest dalesmen in the district, and asked him to tell me what his local knowledge enabled him to tell me about the precise locality of any, or as many, cinder-hills as he was acquainted with. He pointed out the sites of five or six; and then he asked me if I was aware of the 'Roman village' just on the edge of the moor, about half a mile to a mile from where we were talking at the time. I said 'No' in the most natural way I could, and asked him to show me the place. He was delighted to be able to instruct the chief archaelogical authority of the district, and took me 'up the bank', and a pretty steep one it was. On the road thither he showed me one of the cinder-hills he had only indicated by word and gesture previously, and a very nice untampered with specimen of a slag-heap it was, containing I do not know how many hundred tons of slag.

After examining this and making a few local notes, we resumed our climb, and presently came to a large group of pits dotted about in due quincunx order, and in point of numbers such that they might be counted by scores. 'Here they are, sir,' said he, 'and a biggish village it must have been.' I agreed with him. 'But,' I added, 'what makes you call it a Roman village?' – 'Why, sir,' said William, 'there is the "Julius Caesar" band of ironstone there,' pointing to a line easy to be traced in the upper part of the face of the sweeping curve of the bank of the dale-head we had in sight; 'there's the "Julius Caesar" band; and that shows the Romans must have known of it, and named it too.' True, there was the band – more indisputable than the logic perhaps – and the local geologists have named it the 'Julian band'; and tracing the line, it was 'good enough to see', as my friend would have expressed it, that its level was some dozen feet or thereabouts below the surface we were standing on, all pock-marked with my informant's special set of assumed hut-pits.

I am afraid I became chargeable with the crime of perverting my friend William's faith alike in the Romans and their village. My remark was 'Why, it's a bleakish spot, William. It must be a deal snugger and more sheltered down yonder,' pointing to his own home in the valley beneath, – 'especially when it snows and blows in the winter-time; or any time, indeed,' – 'Ay, you may say that,' he replied. 'Well,' I continued, 'but don't you think the Romans were canny enough to have found that out for themselves?' William pondered, perplexed for a while, and then queried with the tone of one 'convinced', but somewhat 'against his will', 'But what do you say them pits is, then, Mr. Atki'son?' The briefest reference to the 'Julius Caesar' band and to the requisite supply of ironstone necessary for the production of the huge mound of slag we had inspected as we came up the hill, lying quite handy seemed to be enough to convert his lingering doubts into a state of quite satisfactory conviction.

Now had Mr Ord been taken to this place in Glaisdale Head, and been duly 'insensed', as I was, there can be little or no doubt, judging from the way in which he deals with similar 'discoveries', that he would at once have discovered another beautiful example of at least a British village; even if the Roman camel was a little in excess of his capacity for absorption. And it is on such foundation, and on no other, that – to mention but two or three of the better-known so-called British settlements – the group of pits above Glaisdale Station, locally known as Holey Intack, the Killing Pits on the verge of the Goathland moors, and the Refholes (as they were called nearly seven hundred years ago) at Westerdale, have been so denominated, or rather nicknamed. So far as I am aware, no particle of actual evidence has ever been offered such as to justify the name in question. The very idea that 'evidence' might be wanted seems never to have entered the mind of the godfathers. Like Caesar, they came, they saw, they conquered; but the conquest they won was localized only in the dreamland of their own fancy. There were the pits; and the pits were of course the sites of ancient British habitation. The process was equally short, summary, decisive, and convincing, so long as no questioning or inquiry was allowed or desired.

Certainly, there are the pits; and if the fiat of the discoverers of British habitations in them be neither like the law of the Medes and

Persians, nor yet absolutely final, the question, 'What, after all, were they?' may be ventured. And this is what a very cautious geological writer has to say about the group last named, – that, namely, at Wester-dale, and situate at no great distance from the village: 'On the northern front of the height called Top End is a considerable plateau constituted of the ironstone and the harder beds of the upper part of the Middle Lias. On this plateau are the 'pits' conjectured by some to be ancient British settlements. These are excavated in the ironstone.' And again, a few pages farther on, he resumes: 'The earliest discoverers of the local stores of ironstone are considered by some to have been the Romans, by others the monks; but we are agreed in thinking that these early operations were carried on in the so-called top seams. With res-pect to the supposed ancient British settlements in Westerdale, which are pits sunk in the main seam of the ironstone, a difference of opinion exists as to the use they may have served.' The writer then proceeds as follows: 'Charcoal is said to have been found at the bottom of some of them, which seems to indicate dwelling-places, yet the great depth seems to militate against the idea.'

Undoubtedly it does; for they are said to be eleven feet deep before the ironstone is reached, and the ironstone itself is two feet thick at the place indicated. And the objection thus raised to the habitation theory – for, however easy it may be to get into a hole eleven or twelve feet deep by as many wide, it might be much less easy to get out of it; to say nothing of the advantages (?) attending the presence of a fire at that depth below the surface – would be quite sufficient to demolish it, even if the finding of charcoal in them – the only item of proof alleged of their occupation as dwellings – were of some little force, instead of being in reality of none at all.

Let me try and illustrate what I mean. I have, I suppose, at one time or another, made intimate acquaintance with the interiors of from one hundred to a hundred and twenty of the grave-hills, little and large, which dot our Cleveland moors all over. But I have never opened one, or seen one opened, in which – although in the larger half of them there were no signs whatever of an interment present – there was not char-coal in noticeable quantities, and in some of the larger houes in such abundance – sometimes in layers covering four or five square feet – as to force attention rather than merely to invite it. And yet I never heard of any one who argued that, simply because of the presence of charcoal, the houes aforesaid were old habitations.

But again, there is another consideration by no means irrelevant to the charcoal incident – and an established fact in the Norfolk flint-pits – and that is this: that at such a depth, even on a not very dark day, especially when the workers had to win the mineral that underlay the circular sides; and still more, when they had occasion to work out what I have called 'the galleries' from the bottom of one shaft to the bottom of its newest or nearest neighbour, artificial light not only may, but must, have been wanted; and it is certainly conceivable that a resinous pine-branch, for instance, may have occasionally done duty in that capacity. And is not this enough to account for the charcoal in the Westerdale and other pits of the same class? The artificial light theory, moreover, does not depend on mere imagination, or even deduction; the flint-tips referred to gave up among other things small-sized lamps rudely fashioned out of the chalk – one or more of them, if I remember, with traces of the wick still in its place.

But indeed the argument from the presence of charcoal to the not-to-be-questioned fact of human residence in the place or places wherein it occurs, is too utterly unreasonable to call for detailed refutation.

To return then to our geological writer (Mr Blake, in *The Yorkshire Lias*): 'On the other hand,' he continues, and that is as militating against the habitation theory, 'there is the remarkable fact of their being excavated on the most considerable outcrop of the ironstone in the dales; and as most other excavations are known to be made for some economical purpose, it would seem probable that these were too. Though the workers would have been very foolish to make such isolated vertical diggings, and not carry their operations horizontally as others have done.'

Yes; but that is the very point to be ascertained, and not gratuitously assumed. So too the isolation is a matter to be ascertained, and not merely assumed. This is what a writer, who in dealing with matters of fact was throughly careful, observant, and accurate – I mean Dr Young, the historian of Whitby – had to say about these pits, in a book published just over seventy years ago: 'The Hole-pits commence about 500 yards south-west of the church, and extend in that direction about 1000 feet, and in breadth about 300 feet. They are partly on the common, but chiefly in an enclosure. The pits are in many places much defaced by the cattle. The most entire are chiefly towards the south end, where some of them owe their preservation to bushes growing on their sides.'

And if some owed their preservation simply to the fortuitous protection afforded by growth of bushes, what about those which had no
such protection? And what about the defacing by cattle, and the ploughing, harrowing, scruffling, tillage generally, within the enclosure? Let
us recall the fact that our own Danby Mine-pit Field has not had a pit
to show within the memory of man, nay, within the date of tradition
even. And while the Westerdale Hole-pits or Refholes are of seven
centuries of ascertained age, it would require a vast deal more proof
than could be adduced that the Mine-pits had not been in process of
working as late as the reign of Henry VII, and possibly even later than
that.

Mr Blake winds up his notice of these Westerdale pits in the following cautious terms: 'Though, therefore, we incline to the opinion that
these may have been early mining excavations, we cannot consider the
fact conclusively proved.' But, at all events, from personal talk with the
writer during the course of his investigations in Westerdale and other
parts of the Danby neighbourhood, I had not the slighest doubt what
his own personal convictions were. And if, on the last day he was at my
house, I could have gone on with him only half a mile farther than the
point to which I had guided him in connection with his ironstone
quest in Fryup, and have told him all I knew only two or three years
later, about Mine-pit Field; or if I could have gone still farther with
him, and showed him what I so soon came to know about as the
'Roman village' and its accompaniments, I dare venture to say that the
sentences quoted above from *The Yorkshire Lias* would have been
very materially altered both in tone and definiteness of assertion.

For my own part, if only the opportunity could be achieved, I
should go in for an examination of any of these so-called British villages
with very definitely preconceived opinions as to what should be looked
for, and the way in which the looking for it should be conducted; and,
for one thing, I should have no more doubt about finding 'horizontal
operations' than about the fact that the pits were there. If I did not find
the ironstone, it would be for precisely the same reason that my geological friend did not find it where 'it ought to have been' just across
the road dividing the old furnaces and slag-heap from the – for our
purpose – happily named 'Mine-pit Field'.

With the Geological Ordnance Survey maps before one's eyes, it is
impossible not to be struck with the fact that there is either a distinctly
marked outcrop of some ironstone seam or band, or else that it is

present at no great depth in the strata marked as those of the surface, in the immediate vicinity of, if not at the precise spot occupied by, every one of the alleged 'villages'. Even at the British village on our Danby north moors, between the Beacon and Waupley – perhaps honoured with more pilgrimages than any other in the list – the tale-telling map places a seam of 'impure ironstone' inconveniently close by. And yet this is the one of all others, the circumstances and surroundings of which admit of most doubt as to their original intention or *raison d'être*. For they are not only not arranged in more or less quincunx order as the rest are (or have been), but they are in two parallel rows, and apparently with an intended outside bank or protection. They have never been properly examined, or indeed subjected to any process of exploration that would satisfy the merest tyro in such inquiries; for the recorded examination already referred to was, as a scientific examination, altogether delusive. True, the inevitable 'bottom' and the inevitable 'charcoal' were found, and the burnt stones, and so forth. But the full and convincing investigation remains to be made; and from my own personal experience on the spot, I am disposed to think that when the true bottom is found the British village theory will be disposed of for good.

Certainly the extravagant absurdity of Mr Ord's account (*Cleveland*, p. 111) might be supposed to have done that already with all thinking readers. If his own words were not reproduced, it might be imagined that I was romancing, not misrepresenting merely; so I give them: 'Our exploration was amply rewarded by the discovery of the remains of a complete BRITISH TOWN of vast magnitude ... stretching upwards of two miles to the base of Rosebury Topping. The remains of these British dwellings are in the form of large oval or circular pits, varying considerably in size, viz. eight to twelve feet deep, and sixty to eighty and a hundred yards in circumference. These pits commence near Highcliff, stretch across Bold Venture Gill and the Kildale road, nearly on a line with Haswell's Hut, run along the lower edge of Hutton Moor, below the Haggs, Hanging-stone, and White Hills, and terminate in a deep line of circumvallation round the upper part of Rosebury Topping. Of the pits here mentioned there are many hundreds in single or double lines, of a zigzag irregular form. ... On one level spot, right of the Kildale road, these habitations are extremely numerous; indeed the hill is completely scooped out like a honeycomb, sufficient to afford room for a whole tribe of Brigantes.' Then come the charcoal, and the burnt stones, and the fortifying, and all the rest of the marvellous tale; but not a thought or a suspicion even of all the strange inconsistencies involved. A 'vast town', 'two miles in length', and – what the adventurous author does not state – following a tortuous course to which the erratic vagaries of a frolicsome letter S, with a curlicue at each termination, would form no unsuggestive parallel, and yet, 'with the comfort of a town', uniting 'the security and protection of a fortified camp'!

But however little our author thought of consistency or possibility, he thought still less of what the geological map, with its perverse system of colouring following all those sinuosities and contortions just noted with a pertinacious fidelity, would have to reveal to an inquirer after the real rather than the fanciful. Even the obliging nomenclators of the Ordnance maps could not quite digest this marvel among discoveries, and they are unkind enough to prefix the word 'supposed' to 'British settlement', and to insert in the very thick of the indications of pits the still unkinder cut involved in the two words 'jet holes'. The simple explanation of course is, that the pits follow the course of the strata containing minerals capable of being applied to economic uses, inclusive of jet as well as ironstone.

Alas for the ruined glory of the 'vast British settlement'!

CHAPTER SEVEN

Hills and Dales

Now, had he chanced one day, when the old woman in question was making bread-cakes for his consumption, and the solitary eye was in the head of the stick (where it used to spend a good half of the four-and-twenty hours) instead of in his own, to stumble as he moved from his place, and in the attempt to steady himself, put his hand by accident upon the cake she was moulding, with the rolling-pin lying across it, the dough would have been impressed with one longitudinal valley, due to the rolling pin, and five smaller ones, roughly at right angles with the long one, and presenting divers irregularities of form and length, due to the eccentric shape and make of the impressed fingers, and, most likely, with some roughnesses and steepnesess here and there, due to the sticking of the paste to the fingers that had not been duly floured before the contact with the dough, and so had broken the smoothness of the edges of the impressions. Now the mould that would thus have been left might serve to give a reasonable idea of the configuration of the district of which Danby forms by far the most considerable part. It must, however, be remembered that the main or rolling-pin valley has a general direction of east and west, and that, consequently, the subsidiary or finger-valleys are roughly north and south. The fifth finger, with its twin tips, will represent Westerdale; the next, Danby-dale; the third, or short middle-finger, Little Fryup; the next, longest of all, Great Fryup; and the remaining one, with its nail rather crushed out of shape, and bulging on the side towards the left hand, Glaisdale. The ridges between the impressions, especially if you bear in mind that the plastic mass of dough, from the nature and manner of pressure put upon it, as supposed, would of necessity thicken towards and beyond the extent of the finger-tips, would represent the moorland ridges which lie between the dales, and which unite beyond the terminations – locally 'the Heads' – of them, forming one huge area of moorland, which grows higher each furlong of its progress towards the south, until, where Danby marches with Rosedale, it reaches at one point the not inconsiderable height of 1420 feet above the sea. But while the impressions of the fingers, such as we have supposed them, with knotty joints and partially distorted configuration, serve fairly well to convey an idea of what these dales are as to fashion and form, we must not suffer ourselves to be entirely misled by the rolling-pin notion. The valley which cuts across the mouths or ends of the dales is no more straight like the pin itself, or regular like its impression, in reality, than the dales themselves are, in proportion as they justify the idea of the impressions made by gouty fingers. It varies in width as it varies in regularity of outline. Some of the outstanding moorland ridges project themselves farther into its area than others do. True, the northern boundary, a bank which rises with decision from the general level of the central valley until it reaches the moor again, and then still goes on ascending until it reaches to nearly 1000 feet above the sea, is much more regular in the directness of its outline than the other side, and is but a little broken in upon by the passage of small streams or 'becks', none of which are of sufficient dimensions to need or produce a dale to convey their waters to the main stream – that, namely, which rolls and rattles, winds and twists its devious course along the slow slope of the central valley. Still, with all these deviations from directness – and in places they are so pronounced that the stream, running past a given point for three-quarters of a mile or so, returns to within a hundred or a hundred and fifty yards of the said point, only to continue the same vagaries at a somewhat lower level – still, with all this, the direction of its course, on the whole, is always to the east, and though it trebles the necessary distance for reaching the place at which it receives the waters of the Glaisdale stream, it receives them at last. And from the vagrant line of this lesser rivulet, called the Glaisdale beck, to the watershed of the ridge between Danby-dale and Westerdale, with a wide deep cantle of moor to the south of the dales, reaching across to Westerdale Head, and with a corresponding sweep of moorland on the north side of the principal valley (claiming a crow-line length of six miles and a half for the extent of its northern boundary), all lies within the meres and limits of the ancient demesne or district known as Danby. The entire area of this great expanse is nearly 23,000 acres of land, of which 11,600 consist of 'undivided moor' belonging to the two townships of Danby and Glaisdale, and 6290 acres represent the enclosed or cultivated land in Danby alone.

No amount of letterpress description can give any adequate idea of what the district really is in its physical aspects and conditions. I once heard a very taking and comprehensively descriptive remark made by a man who had seen much in foreign travel as well as in home rambles, in regard to the diversified sections and aspects of these dales of ours and their characteristic scenery. He said: 'They differ from all other I have ever seen, and in this particular especially, that elsewhere you have to go in search of the beautiful views; here they come and offer themselves to be looked at.' That is true; and necessarily true when the contours and configuration of the district are borne in mind. For the advance or retrocession of a hundred yards or so will remove the obstacle to vision intruded rather than merely presented by some steep nab-end or projecting spur of a hillside outlier, and permit one to gaze at will on some varied or romantic scene alike unexpected and unforeseen.

But even this is but one item in the many which, when united, have the effect of making the Dales scenery what it is. In the way of illustration of what I have just written, I will mention one noteworthy matter. Fryup Head (that is, the upper or higher end of the dale, where it is newest and narrowest, where it has just begun to be scooped out from between its steep containing banks) is one of the most picturesque of all the picturesque dale-heads in the district. At the point at which that division of the dale called 'the head' begins (that is, as you ascend or go up the dale in a southerly direction) the width of the valley from moor edge to moor edge is fully a mile and a quarter. On the west side the upper half of the bank is steep and rocky, and clothed with wood, mainly pines, extending nearly a mile in length. Where the wood ends the last rise or upper hundred feet of the bank becomes more rugged and precipitous, turning round abruptly about the third of a mile farther on, and taking an easterly direction instead of the original one towards the south. And soon after the turn the place or part of the 'head' called 'the hills' is come upon, and 'the hills' in Fryup Head are a very singular feature indeed. Of course the authentic story of the Eildon Hills and the manner of their formation is in everybody's recollection, as are also their general aspect and appearance. Remembering all this, one would be fully justified in assuming that some apprentice of the great manufacturer implicated there had been at work in the head, and that his ''prentice hand' had wanted a very great deal of 'trying' indeed. For all along the last half of the rugged, broken, precipitous bank (as it has now become), spoken of as running towards the east, and yet onwards still, when it makes a turn and goes for the south, lie tumbled, in infinite and most confused confusion, a series of short banklets, hillocks, mounds, and peaks, with intertwining gullies, slacks, and hollows – these last with the lush growth of damp or watery places in them, and the banks with scattered rather than scanty growth of bracken, juniper, and whin all about them. Many a question has been asked me by the people, craving an explanation of this wilderness of confused and tumbled piles of earth and rock. 'Had there been mining, perhaps mining for iron, there, and on a large scale, in old times?' 'Had there been an earthquake, and had it thrown "the hills" up in that strange way?' 'Had they been made and left so by the Flood?' Such questions have been put forth once and again, and I remember wishing the querists could have been present one day as I was walking with an enthusiastic and much-travelled geologist over the lofty ridge of moorland commanding a full view of a great part of these 'hills'. As he came suddenly and unexpectedly in sight of the strange waste of broken ground, down dropped his stick and up went both arms in his surprise and admiration, a rapid exclamation following. 'Oh, what a lovely undercliff!' There was the explanation in one word – an undercliff – and opening up what a vista into the far past! A great body of water filling up these depths that are now dales, in its milder moods gently laving the foot of the cliffs which now supply the moor-topped banks of the dale, and in its rougher tempers sapping their stability as surely as rudely. And then when the process had gone forward to the requisite extent, there ensued the falling forward of the upper and undermined portion – veins of rock and deeper solid beds, and thick strata of unconsolidated earth and stones – and the issue of the fall was 'the hills'.

Strange to say, I once saw these dales – the illusion was so utter, so complete, so perfect, that I can use no other words competent to convey what I want to communicate – I once saw these dales just as they must have appeared in the times – how many tens of thousands of ages ago who shall say? – when this great water-flood filled them. I had been travelling all night in order to get back, after a pressing call from home, to my duty on Sunday. I had left York by the early train, as the trains ran in those days, and there was a trap waiting for me at Grosmont. In this I began my drive, – over moorland almost the whole way when once I had climbed the long wearisome hill from Grosmont Station to the village of Egton. When we reached the heights from which we could see well into Eskdale, it was – so far as the testimony of actual vision went – full of water as far as the eye could see, and full to such a height that only 100 feet or so of the upper banks was not submerged. No amount of rubbing one's eyes prevailed to corroborate the testimony of my recent conviction that there was no water, save the usual fine-weather supply, in the bed of the Esk when I had crossed Grosmont Bridge a short half-hour before. As the scene expanded itself more and more before me, Eskdale and all its tributary dales were inundated, drowned, submerged, and there was the level of the mighty flood just marking its horizontal line at the foot of what ought to have been the higher banks rising from the dales, but which were in all reality, so far as ocular demonstration went, absolute cliffs on the margin of a mighty sheet of water – inlet from the sea or lengthening inland lake. As I mounted higher and higher towards the Beacon, and looked into what ought to have been, and had been, Danby-dale when last I had seen it, there was nothing but the calm glistening surface in sight as far as the eye could discern, and the point I had attained was high enough to enable me to look into the very head of Danby, a good six miles distant. There was a great sheet of water with deep, narrow, far-reaching gulfs or inlets, and only the moorland heights standing out of it. No stranger to the country and to the actual everyday scene could for a moment have suspected that it was not a sheet of water over which his eye roamed.

By this time the sun was getting well up, and there was no cloud to obscure his rising brightness. Truly it was a wonderfully and mysteriously beautiful scene. But just as Nature had spread before our eyes this mimic representation of one of her ancient phases, so Nature presently supplied the disillusionment. As the sun rose to a greater altitude, and his rays began to fall on the seeming water-sheet with incidence at a greater angle, I saw little threads and streaks of the dissembling surface detach themselves from its face, rise up and disappear, like the steam from the locomotive in a fine sunny day. Soon they were followed by larger films. But still the general surface was not visibly affected; until at last, as the process of dissolution continued, a sort of dim translucency seemed to supervene, and the higher range of objects and points, hitherto concealed, began to show themselves, much as if the flood was settling away rapidly, and beginning to leave the trees and higher grounds uncovered. The first object to be seen distinctly was the small group of Scotch pines near the old parish church; the emergence of which was speedily followed by that of the church itself; and then the whole west bank of the dale came into sight; and finally, and almost as if by a species of legerdemain, so rapid and effectual was the process, the whole remaining cumulus of white vapour was caught up, torn to shreds and films, and completely dissipated.

The most typical Dales wedding I ever remember having witnessed was nearly forty years ago and on Martinmas day. But I should not have spoken of the event in the singular number; for there were, in point of fact, four weddings all to be solemnized coincidently. And, whether by arrangement or by chance, all four of the couples, with their attendants, came up to the church in one cavalcade. First, there were no less than seven horsemen, each with a pillion-borne female behind him. Three of these were brides; the others attendants. Of other attendants, male and female, there must have been at least as many more; and then came those who had gathered to see the weddings, and so forth. But besides, there were from a dozen to a score men, mostly young, who carried guns, and who, as the weddingers passed down the little slope leading to the churchyard gate, fired a salvo. As may be supposed, more than one or two of the horses, being neither sobered by age and hard work, nor yet trained to stand fire, were startled and began to plunge or rear. I fully expected a disaster. However, with the exception of one of the pillion ladies, who slid gently – though not without raising her voice – backwards down over the crupper of her steed, no casualty occurred. After the ceremony was over, great was the scramble among the small boys for the coppers, which it was and is customary for the newly married man, or his best man, to scatter the moment the chancel door is left. And then an adjournment to the field adjoining the churchyard was made, and there were a series of races, all on foot, to be run for the ribbons which were the gift of the several brides; and as some of them gave more than one, the races were multiplied accordingly.

Time was, and not so very long before the commencement of my incumbency here, when these races were ridden on horseback; and at an earlier period still, the race was a 'steeple-chase' across country – the goal being the house whence the bride had come, and to which the wedding cavalcade was to return for the usual festivities. More than once, too, I have known, when the bride in some way incurred the suspicion of niggardliness, through not complying with the recognized usage of supplying one ribbon at least to be run for, the 'stithy was fired upon her', *i.e.* a charge of powder was rammed into a hole in the anvil (much after the fashion of a 'shot' in a mine) and fired in derision; well pronounced, if the loudness of the report counted for anything; as the wedding party passed on the journey home from the church. The direct converse of this, was the firing of guns as the party passed the residences of friends or well-wishers.

The almost invariable practice on the part of the newly married man has been, and still is, after the registration in the vestry has been duly attended to, and when the party are just on the point of leaving the church, to hand to the officiating minister, nominally in payment of the fees, a handful, sometimes a very large handful, of money, taken without the slightest pretence of counting it from his trousers pocket, from which the said minister is expected to take the usual fees for parson and clerk; and, that done, to hand over the surplus to the bride. Twice within my incumbency a deviation from this ritual – and a very pretty deviation – had occurred. The bridegroom, together with the ring, at the proper point in the service, has laid upon the book the aforesaid handful of money, so that, besides the direct pertinency of the next following part of the service, viz. 'With this ring I thee wed,' ensued a typification of the further sentence, 'With all my wordly goods I thee endow'.

The races still linger on, and only a week or two since the bride gave two 'ribbons to be run for'; and a few years ago one young chap, fleet of foot, and with as much inclination for 'laiking' (playing) as for sticking to work – some folk said more – was quoted as the fortunate winner of almost enough to start an itinerant haberdasher in trade. But still, even so, 'what a falling off was there!' For nearly the whole, if not the whole of the usages under notice are, in the strictest sense, survivals. To what an extent the original customs obtained in the district may be as largely, as well as safely, inferred, perhaps, from the memorials engraved on the tablets of the folk-speech, as from any other source or authority. There are three terms, of which it is almost incorrect to say that, however much fallen into disuse, they are quite obsolete. These are, Bride-ale, Bride-door, Bride-wain; and they are defined, the first, as 'the warmed, sweetened, and spiced ale yet presented in some villages to a wedding party on its return from church'; the second, as 'the door of the house from which the bride proceeds to church, and at which the wedding festivities are to be held afterwards: used in the phrase "to run for the bride-door"'; and the third, as 'a waggon, loaded with household goods, to be conveyed from the bride's father's house to the bridegroom's.' The late F. K. Robinson, the careful compiler of the Whitby Glossary, and collector of unconsidered trifles in the way of tradition, local legend, and the like, says, 'To "run for the bride door" is to join in the race for the bride's gift, run by divers of the young men of the neighbourhood, who wait near the church-door till the marriage ceremony is over. The prize is usually a ribbon, which is worn for the day in the hat of the winner.'

Hardly more than half a century since these races were hotly contested in Danby by mounted men, two or three of whom, together with their steeds, were well known for their exploits on such occasions of racing. One of these men, a member of an old and 'yabble' (well-to-do) Danby family, was, if my memory serves me rightly, the retailer of a tradition, mentioned for my instruction, that in days gone by the race was always from the churchyard gate to the bride-door, and that the prize was not barely the bride's garter, but the added privilege of taking it himself from her leg as she crossed the threshold of her home. The hot-pots of the Cleveland dales, the liberal ale-drinking in Cumberland and Craven, the rapid riding as well as the fact of the mounted caval-cade, all point to Northern customs, where the very word for a wedding – *brullaup*, or bride-rush or speed – is itself a standing testimony to what the marriage ride was in the old days; and as to that, let the following sentence bear its own witness: 'The most ancient mode of wooing had at least the merit of simplicity; it consisted in carrying off the desired object by physical force. There are traces of the custom in a ceremony still occasionally practised on the marriage of a Welsh peasant. After the wedding the bridegroom mounts on horseback and takes his bride behind him. A certain amount of "law" is given them, and then the guests mount and pursue them. It is a matter of course that they are not overtaken; but, whether overtaken or not, they return with their pur-suers to the wedding feast.' The old usage in vogue when the matter in hand was the obtaining of a helpmeet amid the burdens and labours of life, which lives as a survival in the old classical myth of the Rape of the Sabines, – the usage which prescribed or compelled the securing of a spouse by an absolute abduction of her by force from another tribe or another district – is more than faintly figured forth in the Welsh cus-tom just named, while the horse-races of two or three generations back, explained by all we now know concerning the marriage customs of the remote past, contain much more than an indication merely of what their real origin and meaning unquestionably must be. And, little as the fleet-footed young dalesmen think of it when 'running for the ribbon', they are doing their little best to keep up the remembrance that, in the old days of their fore-elders' and predecessors' living experience, if a man wanted a wife, he had to go and seek her where it was known there was an eligible young lady, who might be won literally *vi et armis*, or by dint of the strong hand and fleet enduring horse.

As to the bride-wain the thing may be obsolete, but neither the feeling nor the practice connected with the name is so. The long lists of 'wedding presents' we see paraded in the newspapers on occasion of some 'high-up' bridal, and the array of less gorgeous but equally well-intended presents one may see in even our humble Dales habitations, alike testify to the survival of the idea which found its expression in the older days in the bride-wain and its accessories.

As to what the bride-wain really was. When I first came into residence here, there were few farmhouses in which there was not one of those fine old black oak cabinets or 'wardrobes', with carved panels, folding-doors, and knobby feet, that have gladdened so many collectors' hearts; in not a few cases I have seen them in old cottages also. And not once or twice only, but many times I have heard the name 'bride-wain' attributed to them. The word itself was sufficient to suggest if not to provoke inquiry. For the 'wain' was a vehicle that went upon wheels, and upon two wheels rather than four; because the wain upon four wheels speedily became a waggon, and ceased to be a wain. But a press or wardrobe certainly is not a vehicle, however much it may be a repository.

But the wardrobe might be, and often was in the olden times, a constituent portion of the 'wedding presents', which always partook of the homely and useful character, almost to the exclusion of the merely graceful or pretty, and much more the sentimental. And the closets above, with their carven doors, and the drawers below with their antique brass handles and lock-plates, so far from being empty, were uncomfortably full with articles of household garnishing or personal wear, made from home-grown, home-spun, home-woven, home-made material, linen or woollen. Much thereof might be the work of the bride's own deft, if toil-hardened fingers; but much, too, came of the many and heartily offered gifts of the neighbours and friends of the young couple. And it was once a thing of occasional occurrence rather than a custom that could be said to prevail, to place this wardrobe, so stored, on a wain – itself a gift like the rest, as well as the oxen which drew it – and convey it to the church at which the marriage ceremony was to be solemnized; making it a part of the wedding procession, in fact, and letting it stand by the church-door, or in the very porch, while the priest was fulfilling his function; and after the service to drag it thence to the future abode of the couple just made one. So by an easy transition of idea the wardrobe itself came to be called a bride-wain. 'One such bride-wain', I have said in my Glossary, 'which took its departure for the church from Danby Castle, was specially mentioned by my informant as having had no less than sixteen oxen yoked to it', many of the oxen so employed having actually been gifts (as noticed above), as well as the wardrobe itself, and no small part of its contents.

I remember having an old man of nearly seventy pointed out to me in my father's Lincolnshire parish, who was said to own land and property to the value of a thousand pounds or so, and of whom it was told that, on coming away from the church on his wedding-day, he said to his newly-made wife, 'I have the price of a pint still left in my pocket. Shall we go to the public-house and drink it, or shall we go and work?' And the lady was said to have answered, 'Well, if it is left to me, I say, let us work,' and work they did; and they worked on from his two-pence halfpenny to his thousand. I think there was the same downright and honest thrift and perseverance and industry throughout these dales in the old days; and I think, too, it was better than the aping of the 'wedding-tour' which is now getting the upper hand.

CHAPTER EIGHT

Graves Ancient and Recent

I THINK I have had, first and last, within the last five-and-twenty years, either shown me or brought to me, something like a large wheelbarrow-load of fragments of pottery taken out of the earth thrown up in the process of digging the necessary graves in the Danby churchyard. It is mainly of one character – coarse, rough, and red; red, however, of different shades. Most of the vessels of which these sherds are fragments seem to have been of the jug or pitcher description, having handles, plain or lined or twisted, with mouths, not of large size in proportion to the other dimensions, flanging outwards a little, and glazed inside for some little depth, and with the glaze in some instances straying a little over the outside of the neck.

That these vessels are of mediaeval date there can be no doubt. Precisely similar vessels – similar, that is, as to ware, colour, shape or average form, handles, glaze, etc. – may be seen in any collection of such pottery, notably in the York Museum.

I have, in some cases, seen portions of five or six different specimens taken out of the earth thrown up from one grave; and in very few instances indeed is a grave dug without the occurrence of some of these reminiscences of a past and forgotten usage.

But besides these old sherds, there is disclosed in almost every case more or less charcoal, sometimes in quantities such as to attract the trained eye at once, and always in particles the size of a small bean, or in small sections, admitting of easy identification when looked for. I have occasionally seen half a spade-graft of mould brought to the surface, nearly one-half or one-third of which was composed mainly of charcoal. In fact my sexton – who was trained to the watchful part of the barrow work, so that he became one of two best men – still lives in hope of finding such a mass of charcoal in connection with the pottery as to enable us to come to a satisfactory conclusion touching the presence of the substances throughout the churchyard.

It was but the other day that, in the course of my casual reading, I met with the record of a silver coin being found still between the jaws of the skull of a man who had been buried three centuries or more ago, and it reminded me of what had happened at one of the churches in this neighbourhood not twenty years since, as far as my recollection serves me. On the disturbance and removal of the remains of a former interment, when the skull came to be moved something was heard to rattle in among the bones of it, which, on examination, proved to be a silver coin about the size of a Commonwealth half crown (or rather florin, I suppose). And it was evident that its original place of deposit must have been between the teeth, or at least just inside the mouth.

One of my earliest recollections as a boy is of places – houses, always old and mostly old-fashioned, barns, lanes, the moated sites of old manor houses, 'four want-ways' or the place of intersection of two cross roads, churchyards, suicides' graves – which were spoken of, dreaded, avoided after nightfall, as being 'haunted'. There were two barns, one local 'hall', one moated site of an old mansion, one road-side grave, all within half an hour's walk of one of my homes in the days of my boyhood, besides a long disused old house of considerable size and pretension, a grove, and an old ruinous building, which once, I suppose, had been the parish pest-house, close to the place of my school-days – to say nothing of a long, dark passage behind two of the dormitories at the school itself – all of which were 'haunted'. And there was a large section of an old moated mansion in another of my father's curacies, with a tapestried chamber in it, the subject illustrated thereon being the beheading of John the Baptist, with his bleeding head in the charger, wrought in right grisly fashion; as to which I heard a man, mainly employed in my father's garden, tell a right gruesome story of his own experiences there one night when storm-stayed.

I found no difficulty in entering into the feelings of the narrator, and understanding the impression produced upon him. And perhaps I was enabled to trace the mental process throughout; for the district he lived in was full of common place, unimaginative superstition. But there is no need to give a catalogue of the apparitions, ghosts, spirits, which were said to beset the district, or to enter into exhaustive details. A sample or two will suffice. There was a lady who, at a certain hour on a certain night, depending on the moon's age, walked abroad in her blood-stained night-gear, but without her head. There was another of the same sex, and habited also in her white night-gown, who 'walked' with her hands chained and her lower limbs fettered, sobbing and crying, and jangling her chains. There was the great dog *minus* his head, who ran to his destination – where he vanished suddenly – as well as if he had his eyes in the usual place to guide him. There was the black wide-horned creature with great glaring saucer eyes, at the old moat. There was the shape of the suicide, with his self-murdering knife, his gibbering features, trembling limbs, and pitiful moans – all of these, and many more. And the story was, this man had cut his own throat, and by 'crowner's-quest law' had been buried by the roadside with a stake driven through his body. I make no doubt all that was true to the letter. And then there had been a jumbling together of the old tradition and of older folklore ideas, which had got mixed in the process, and the issue or the process was the ghost.

There is no doubt that the self-murderer, or the doer of some atrocious deed of violence, murder, or lust, was buried by some lonely roadside, in a road-crossing, or by the wild woodside, and that the oak, or oftener, thorn stake was driven through his breast; but not because of any intended scorn, or horror, or abhorrence. These were the characters who – to use an expression common enough among us to this day, though perhaps we do not trouble to think of its origin or meaning – could not 'rest in their graves'. They *had* to wander, nay, often they were self-constrained to wander about the scenes of their crimes, or the places where their unhallowed carcases were deposited, unless, that is to say, they were prevented; and as they wanted the semblance, the *simulacrum*, the shadow-substance of their bodies for that purpose – otherwise there could have been no appearance – the body it was which was made secure by pinning it to the bottom of the grave by aid of the driven stake. Here is an explanation which has long been lost sight of, and replaced by notions involving the ideas of ignominy, abhorrence, execration, or what not; and it is just the explanation that was wanted. The corpse of the fearful malefactor, cast out of hallowed ground, as belonging to the devil and not to the saints, must be disabled, as well as the guilty spirit itself, for further mischief or ill-doing.

And there were other means adopted with the same end in view. The head was severed from the body and laid between the legs, or placed under the arm – between the arm and the side, that is. Or the feet and legs were bound together with a strong rope. Or the corpse might be cut up into some hollow vessel capable of containing the pieces, and carried away quite beyond the precincts of the village and deposited in some bog or morass, so as never to come within the precincts of the hallowed ground.

Now these things are not the creation of fancy. The records of such sentences and of their execution exist in the Dooms-books or other judicial records of this country and other lands in the north of Europe, and there is a sort of uncanny recognition in them of the apparitions of headless ladies and chain-rattling ghosts, ghastly bearers of cruel knives and the like.

I remember when, some twenty-five years or more ago, I became acquainted with Hylten Cavallius's admirable book on the ethnology of a certain district in the south of Sweden, I was greatly struck with the passage of which the following is a translation: 'For the purpose of preventing restless, unruly, sinful, and intensely worldly men from "going again after death" ' – the Cleveland idiom is 'coming again' – 'our Wärend folk have been in the habit from a very remote time of employing various characteristic measures. The very oldest among these takes its origin from the ancient fire-cult, and the still older sun-worship. It is to this that we must refer the presence, for the protection of the dwelling against ghosts (*gengångare*), of a red cock, the solar bird, on his perch over the house-entrance. To the same again must be referred the custom of consuming with fire the mattress on which a man has breathed his last; of casting live coals (charcoal, notably) after a corpse on its removal from the dwelling, and of strewing ashes, salt, linseed, or the seed of the water-hemlock, around the homestead, or across the approach to the house, beyond which limit the ghost may not pass. On the same principle, subsequently to the time at which men became acquainted with the use of steel, the custom has been to drive in an axe or some other sharp-edged tool above the door of the house-place. And at a later period still it became usual to tie the feet of the corpse together, to stick pins into the shroud in such wise that the points were opposed to the feet; as also to place hooks and eyes in the coffin, or else a stake wrenched out of the fence round the homestead. Moreover, when a corpse is carried out of the house of death, it is invariably borne forth feet first, in order to prevent the dead person from "coming again". Nay, even in the days of hoary eld, it was a custom to whisper in the ear of the corpse that he was not to "come again"; while, finally, there was the old practice of laying earth on the body, which was a heathen practice long before it was adopted in the Christian grave-service. And even yet the accustomed Wärend name for the burial ceremony is to "earth-fasten a corpse", or to "earth-fasten the dead person".'

Turning all this over in one's mind, and remembering at the same time that the idea represented by the word 'haunted' is as yet by no means an extinct idea, there is no great difficulty in suggesting an explanation of the presence of charcoal in these old graves in the churchyards.

But it is possible to illustrate the living reality of this superstition by a reference to what took place here not so very long before my personal acquaintance with the place commenced. An old woman who lived in Fryup, and whose chief celebrity depended upon the allegation that she kept the 'Mark's e'en watch', and was able in consequence to fore-show the deaths of the coming year, one St. Mark's day, when she was questioned on the subject after her vigil, announced her own death as among the foredoomed ones, and assigned her reason for saying so. 'And,' she added, 'when I dee, for dee I s'all, mind ye carry me to my grave by t' church-road, and not all the way round by t' au'd Castle and Ainthrop. And mind ye, if ye de'ant, I'll come again.'

Now the church-road lay straight past her house to the foot of a very steep moor-bank, up which it went – and goes yet – with two zigzags. It is a stiff climb at any time, even when one has only himself and his coat to carry; but with a burden such as a coffin, with the grisly occupant inside, it is 'hosses' wark, not men's'. Well, the old lady died as she had predicted, and she died in a snowy time. And the difficulties of the church-road in a snowy time are almost intensely enhanced. I have gone both up and down the bank at such seasons, and speak with feeling. But the bearers faced the difficulties – perils, in a sense, they almost amounted to – and waist-deep sometimes; still they persevered, and eventually got through with their undertaking and their burden. In plain words, they were ready to face anything; and many among them must have had such a day of toil and effort and fatigue as never before nor after fell to their lot; but they could not, dared not, face the chance of the old woman's 'coming again'.

My own idea, entertained now for a very long time past, relatively to the presence of charcoal and broken pottery in our graves, is that they were placed at the first in the original graves in conjunction; that is to say, the charcoal, in the form of live coals, was placed inside the earthen vessels. And while it is possible that the purificatory energy of

fire may not have been lost sight of in the observance, all the pro-
babilities suggested by such collateral items of evidence as those I have
quoted go to show that the deposit was of the nature of the casting of
live embers after the departing corpse, burning the straw mattress on
which the departed had given up the ghost, strewing ashes, salt, or what
not, or striking some sharp-edged instrument above the house-door,
with the avowed object of keeping ghosts, or *the* special ghost, in
abeyance. And at this point there is another fact which it will be by no
means irrelevant to advert to. And that is, that in all the burial mounds
I have myself opened or seen opened, or the opening of which as
described by competent observers, taking special notes of all incidental
and collateral particulars I am acquainted with, I do not remember an
instance in which the absence of charcoal is recorded. I do not mean that
there was always such evidences of burning as are attested by the
presence of charcoal in mass, or sensible quantities, but that the unvary-
ing rule appears to be that charcoal occurs in all these mounds, scattered
up and down throughout the greater part of the hill. Even in the small
houes, fifteen to twenty feet across, and a foot and a half, or little more,
in height (of which literally hundreds have existed on these moors, and
many scores of which are still in being, and none of which ever covered
a burnt body), there are small fragments of charcoal in every individual
mound, varying in size from a bean to a nutmeg, far more than enough
to convey the inevitable conclusion that it was not there accidentally.

The speculation, the corroborative considerations, and the conclusion as to the why and because of the occurrence of charcoal and
potsherds in our Danby graves, are all, whether entertained or no,
matters of no slight or merely local interest.

I hardly cared to enter upon my recollections or experiences in relation
to the peculiarities which have characterized Danby funerals – or, to use
the older Cleveland word, 'burials' – some of which even yet are hardly
things of the past, without first adverting to the occurrence of both
charcoal and broken pottery, in marked quantity, in the oft-stirred
earth thrown up in the process of digging our modern graves. That
occurrences of this kind are not exceptional, that they are not confined
to Danby alone, I am well aware. I have never examined the earth
thrown out of a new-made grave in any one of the churchyards of the
near district without finding samples of the pottery; and I will specify
the churchyards of Great Ayton, Westerdale, and Sneaton as among

those most prominent in my recollections. I have also heard the same of one or two other churchyards wherein I have had no opportunity of personal examination. One other remarkable case, however, is almost worth special notice.

Many years ago I had undertaken a week-day service in the school-room at Dunsley. In some way or other, after the service, the subject of graveyard potsherds was referred to, and the schoolmaster remarked that he had collected a number of such fragments, which appeared to answer the description I had been giving. He produced a quantity of them, and without exception they were similar to those with which I was so familiar, except only that they were all portions of broken pot- or pitcher-handles. But on inquiry, it proved that these only had been preserved, because they were not mere sherds from the broken sides of the vessels. I further learned that all came from a place in the close vicinity of the school, namely, the site of the ancient Dunsley chapel. I went with the master to the place, and he showed me where the greater part had been met with, and although he did not seem very hopeful that renewed search would be successful, still certain small pieces were found. I will only add that my informant made no doubt about the sherds coming from the old graves; and old graves they certainly were. Young's memorandum concerning the old chapel is as follows: 'It was older than the Hermitage of Mulgrif, and it subsisted longer; for it continued until the Dissolution'; and in a note he adds: 'An imperfect inscription shows that it had been used as a cemetery prior to the Reformation. ... The foundation of the north wall has been undermined by people digging up materials for repairing roads, and the bones of the dead have been exposed to view.'

But truly the 'burials' were rather a thorn in my side for long. It is almost 'a tale that is told' now, but it is perhaps worth recalling and recording. As soon after the breath had left the body as was possible, the next day at the latest – often the same day, if the person had died early – the person whose professional name was 'the bidder', went round from house to house among those who were to be 'bidden to t' burial', to 'warn' them that the burial was fixed for such and such a day, and to add, 'and so and so' – naming the principal friend or friends of the deceased – 'expect you at ten o'clock in the morning'. The 'minister' was always among the first to be bidden. Sometimes when the dead person had been long in the place, had borne parochial office, and had won the goodwill and respect of all the neighbours, or if he was a man with numerous relations and connections (a very common case), or for whom general sympathy had been aroused, these invitations might be numbered, not merely by the score, but by the hundred. I have myself counted more than three hundred seated in the church on at least four, if not five, different occasions. And the rule is, and, still more, was, that the preponderating majority of these 'went to the burial' at the house where the corpse lay, beginning at ten o'clock and continuing to drop in, according to convenience or distance to be traversed, throughout the morning and afternoon till it became time to 'lift the body' and make a start for the church.

And all these were fed – entertained, rather – at the house of mourning, if it chanced to be that of one of the principal inhabitants. All day long, in relays of from a dozen up to a score, according to the dimensions of the reception-room, the hungry host came streaming in, until all had been 'served'. Those who had been the first to enter went and sat about wherever they could find seats, whether in the house or outside, or in the farm premises, or at some neighbour's, smoking (not without the necessary 'wet', it might be) and chatting, as on any other occasion when friends and acquaintants were wont to meet. The last part of the entertainment, at least in the later days of the old practice, was to hand round on salvers or trays glasses of wine and small round cakes of the crisp sponge description, of which most of the guests partook.

As to the preparation made for supplying the bodily wants of such great concourses, I have again and again heard statements made as to the number of 'stones of beef and ham' provided and consumed. Notably this was so in the case of one of the worthiest of the many worthy Dales yeomen – 'freeholders', they call themselves – it has been my privilege as well as my pleasure to know, who was one of the churchwardens when I came here, and who died at the age of eighty-eight, never having paid a doctor's fee up to his death-illness, which was rather cessation of life than sickness. When he was buried, between two and three hundredweight of meat, mainly beef and bacon, was put on the tables; and when the keeper and owner of one of the inns at Castleton died – a man universally popular as well as known to all – the amount provided was said to have been even greater still.

These great assemblages and colossal providings are now mainly things of the past, although even within the past year I have twice seen upwards of one hundred and fifty to two hundred persons assembling or assembled in the church and churchyard to be present at a funeral.

Necessarily when there were such numbers of friends and relations to be fed, and such scant accommodation as cramped space in the kitchen, as well as at the board, entailed, there was great loss of time, and often exceeding unpunctuality in the starting, and, much more, the arrival at the churchyard of the funeral cortege. Once in my predecessor's time the arrival did not take place until after dark, and the service in the church – which is near no house at all save one, and that is a third of a mile distant – had to be read by the light of a tallow dip, procured after some delay, and the grave-side service by the wavering, flickering light of the same held in the sexton's hand.

Delay too would naturally in such a district as ours be caused by distance and bad roads; and other causes also led to unpunctuality. For in one case, when the funeral was fully two hours late, the procession had started in ample time, and the detention had arisen from a totally unforeseen and, in practice, unaccustomed cause. It was a long way that had to be traversed, undoubtedly – nearer twelve than ten miles, I should say – and much more than half of it over highways that crossed the moors. Yet there was a short cut that might have been taken, but was not taken, contrary to the intentions and expectations of the organizer of the journey. For on reaching the point of divergence from the accustomed way, or the 'highway', the proposed deviation was at once demurred to, and in the issue a sort of parliament was held on the high-road, and the decision to proceed by the high-road was deliberately come to.

And why? Nobody doubted that to take the longer way round would add still more to the delay occasioned by the debate; but there was a graver consideration than that, and one with which the weightier part of the mourners could not and would not deal lightly. The person to be buried was no other than the man previously mentioned more than once in these pages, namely, our friend Jonathan, who had fought the witches so strenuously with the best weapons at his command. 'Take Jonathan to his last house otherwise than by the "church-road" Why, it wasn't to be thought of! He would never rest in his grave. He would come again. Didn't every one know that such as were carried to the church otherwise than by the "church-road" were provoked, and got the power to come again?'

But there are yet other matters to be remarked, or our notice of the observances at a Dales 'burying' would be left imperfect. Thus the

coffin is never borne on the shoulders of the bearers, as is most customary elsewhere. So far as it is 'carried by hand' at all – which, from the
distance of the church from all the constituents of the population, is
very little, usually only from a few yards outside the churchyard-
gate to the trestles set to support it in the western part of the nave of
the church – it is carried by the aid of towels knotted together and passed
under the coffin, the ends on either side being held by the bearers, six
in number (or three pairs). And as regards the bearers, the usage was so
consistent and so steadfast that there would be no impropriety in speaking of it as 'the rule'. Thus a single young woman was borne by six
single young women, a single young man by six of his compeers, a
married woman by married women, and so on all through. Nay, it is no
unusual sight even yet to see the child carried by six children, varying
according to the sex of the dead child. In the case of the young un-
married woman, moreover, some peculiarities of costume were always
to be observed about the bearers. Their dress was not all unrelieved
black. White sashes or scarfs were customarily worn, and white gloves
always. Much of this remains still, but the observance in such matters is
hardly so religious as it used to be.

CHAPTER NINE

Dogs in Church

FORTY years ago the 'Dog-whipper' was still an institution in this dale. Auld Willy Richardson was then the hereditary holder of the office, his father having been dog-whipper before him; and when Willy himself died, the office, the honour, and the insignia passed to his brother John. For the office was by no means one without outward signs and tokens of its existence. The office-holder held also a whip, and whenever he was on duty the whip was *en évidence*.

Poor old Willy, the first dog-whipper of my acquaintance, was a little man of about five feet four, with legs that were hardly a pair, and which it would have been slander to call straight or well shapen; and, as was natural perhaps, he shambled in his gait. His usual garb on the Sunday was an ancient drab coat, cut – if a tailor had ever been concerned in the making of it – after the fashion described as that of Dominie Sampson's, with broad skirts falling quite below the knee. There were side-pockets in it, opening just upon the hip; capacious and with a sort of suggestiveness about them that they were not simply meant to contain sundries, but were put to such a use by wont and custom. On Sundays, and days when a 'burying' was to be – for Willy was sexton also, and kept the depth of his graves religiously to under three feet – the short handle of the whip he bore reposed in the right-hand pocket, but the lainder and lash hung outside; the latter, inasmuch as the bearer's stature was not great, trailing on the ground.

Willy was valorous in the execution of his duty, although he may sometimes have seen occasion for the exercise of a wise discretion. I knew of two such instances. In one the intrusive dog was made slowly to recede before the duly-armed official, who was fairly well able to command the whole interspace between the pews which runs the length of the church; but when it came to turning round the corner and backing towards the door, the dog did not see the expediency of the desired course quite so clearly as Willy did; and so, having more room in the crossing in which to attain the necessary impetus, he made a bolt for it, aiming at the archway presented by the dog-whipper's bow-legs. But the archway proved to be less than the dog had assumed it to be; and, in consequence, after riding backwards for a pace or two, poor old Willy came backwards to the pavement, and to grief besides. The dog on the other occasion was more resolute, or else less accommodating; for he met all Willy's advances with a steady refusal to budge an inch in a backward direction. Willy persevered; the dog growled. Willy showed his whip; the dog showed his teeth; and the teeth having a more persuasive look about them than the whip, the man gave way and the dog did not.

Willy Dog-whipper's successor, as I have said, both as to the office and its badge, was his brother John. Him I induced, by the addition of sixpence from the parson's magnificent burial-fee of eightpence, to his own pittance of one shilling and threepence for digging the grave, attendance at the funeral, and filling up the grave at the close, to dig the graves an extra foot in depth. But it was an innovation to which, despite the – by comparison – easily earned sixpence extra, he never completely grew reconciled. He thought a coffin with twenty or twenty-two inches of soil upon it was 'weel eneugh happed oop for owght'. John wore a ring, made out of the old coffin-tyre he met with in digging the graves in the well-worked churchyard the Danby 'kirk-garth' was, until I got an additional half acre laid to it. This ring was good against 'falling fits'. His predecessor's particular wear had been earrings of the same material.

These two worthies held other offices, either by favour or by inheritance or descent. Willy was the 'bidder to the burials', while John was in extensive request on occasions of pig-killing; and, having a considerable number of patrons and friends among the farmers, and others who had pigs to kill in the course of the winter, he had very many engagements of that kind. It was said that, in addition to his food and a small money fee on these occasions, he had the pigs' ears as his perquisite; and that he always kept count of how many pig executions he had attended in the course of the season, by aid of small reserved and preserved pieces of the said ears.

But there was a matter to be noted in connection with this family which may be more worth recording than any yet mentioned. Besides the aforesaid Willy and John, there was a sister, Nanny, who would assuredly have been credited with the character of a witch had she lived two or three generations earlier, and have met with the observance usual in such cases. In fact, there were some whose opinions on that subject were not quite settled, as it was. Not three months since I was asked, 'Had she not had that reputation?' This woman, a good match in symmetry and size to her brother Willy, was, during the greater part of her life, after my acquaintance with her began, practically voiceless. She could not even so much as whisper audibly; and it did wear an uncanny look to see her, so to speak, trying to talk – lips, mouth, tongue in rapid motion, and with a sort of emphatic action – and yet not be able to hear a sound. Some even of my own children thought her alarming, and were shy of being accosted by her. But the noteworthy matter remaining to be chronicled in connection with her, and certainly one of her brothers, if not both, was that practically they lived by begging. But that expression must not be misunderstood. They were not professional mendicants; but they were the survivals, and the last survivals, of an outworn system. Thus Nanny, to the last day of her life and ability to go her accustomed rounds, had her dinner one day in the week at one particular farmhouse, and another dinner another day at another house; and besides this she had 'a piece' here and 'a piece' there given her, to carry away in her bag for home consumption. The system is, of course, utterly obsolete now, and in England generally it has been so for long. But it was an accredited system once; and I think accredited by at least unwritten law as well as custom. What I mean will appear from the following extract from the Orders made at Quarter Sessions held at Thirsk, 4th April, 1654: 'In regard the parishioners of Osmother-ley withdraw their charitie, which formerly they gave at their doores to Alexander Swailes, a poor man, it is therefore Ordered that the parish officers there shall, for the future, pay the said poor man 12d. weekly.' Our parishioners here did not 'withdraw their charitie' from poor, voiceless old Nanny up to something more than twenty years ago. I buried her in 1867, and as long as she was able to walk about I used to meet her with her accustomed bag, and knew she had a place reserved for her once a week at Howe End.

One of my old parishioners who I called Frank and, for whom I entertained lively feelings of regard and attachment – died of consumption some twelve or fifteen years ago.

One day when I was talking to Frank about many things, one of us adverted to some notice or other which had recently been going the round of the papers about a toad found enclosed in the boll of an old tree, which was being split up (or cut up) for firewood, or something of that sort; and Frank asked me what my opinion was as to the rights in that much-vexed question. I expressed my unqualified incredulity, both as to the alleged fact itself and as to the authenticity of the statements in regard to it. But Frank did not take my view, that was clear. He did not see why it could not be. 'Why, pricky-back othcins (urchins, hedgehogs) slept all the winter thruff (through), and he himself had offens seen the backbearaways (bats) hinging up in the church-tower, and au'd garrets i' different spots, and a few weeks more or less of winter seemed to make no differ to thae; and besides folks did say that swallows had been fished up out of the bottoms of ponds and such like, all hinging together like bees iv a swarm, and all as wick (alive) as gam'-some kitlins (frolicsome kittens).' But I saw there was more in my companion's mind than even these natural history recollections, and after a little trouble I got him to tell me what it was. He believed toads could live, and did live, 'a weight of years even', if they happened to be covered up, ay, and blocked up so they couldn't stir and much more get out. 'Why, he had heared thae teeads (toads) that had been covered up years and years ago, with loads of broken stone, rubble, earth, old mortar — all sike-like minglements as came in mason-work, from pulling down old buildings and putting up new — five foot deep in some places; and yet he had heard them croaking, not once or twice only, but scores of times; and that showed they could live in such spots.' And nothing could shake this good man's faith that the toads he had heard were the toads whose dwelling-place he had helped to fill up so many years before.

I do not for a moment doubt that my poor friend had heard the croakings in question, nor even that they had come from the place he affirmed them to have come from. I no more disbelieved his statement than I disbelieved the evidence of my own eyes one day when, amid a little scene of excitement among my fellow-workers, I saw a living viper disclosed from a pile of stonework in the heart of a barrow on the moor, which stonework lay below a superincumbent covering of earth at least two feet in thickness. But then I could account for the presence of the toads where Frank said he had heard them just in the same way as I could account for the presence of the hagworm three or four feet below the surface of the houe. Some means of entrance and access to the interstices between the piled stones existed in either case, although it escaped notice, and even suspicion, in the case of all the observers, myself only excepted. It is the habit of the toad, equally with the viper, to 'choose for its winter retreat some retired and sheltered hole, a hollow tree, or a space amongst large stones, or some such place', as Mr Bell writes, and so the old habitat below the castle would still be occupied during the winter, and when the spring came again, and the toads awaked from their long slumber, they would be likely to croak as naturally as a man yawns under the like circumstance every morning.

I do not like to misuse the words fancy and imagination. The latter is a grand thing, and the other a pleasant thing. And so I do not care to say, 'What a lot of imagination or what an amount of fancy is expended upon very everyday topics connected with natural history!' but I would rather say, 'What an awful lot of unthinking, unstable supposings or assumings, based upon no real or genuine observation, is continually put forward in almost every vehicle of natural history "Notes and Queries"!' and my dearly-beloved starlings are among the sufferers thereby.

A few years ago there was a craze among some fancy ornithologists to make the cock starling a bigamist. Positively the theory was started that he customarily had a couple of hens attached to him, and that this accounted for the groups of three one perpetually saw in the breeding time! For one thing, although I have been on very intimate terms with starlings for some sixty years, I did not even know that 'groups of three' were to be recognized at all. Certainly I have often seen three together, but the same observation holds good of most other species of birds, I think; but as to a male starling mating with two female starlings at one and the same time, the idea is simply absurd to any one who has the opportunity, continued for dozens of years, of watching all the domestic proceedings of some ten or twelve pairs of the birds in question during the entire breeding season; five to seven of their nests, moreover, being placed within three yards of his seat by his own dining-room window.

Starlings 'pair', literally and simply; and if I were asked to give the impressions produced in my own mind by what I have observed in connection with my own private colony here especially, I should say that I am by no means sure they do not remain paired all the year round – at least in some cases. Thus, they always come back to their haunts in the ivy surrounding their nesting-boxes, and they always come in even numbers. To avoid begging the question, I say – not that there are three pairs, but – six birds here now, and for the last six weeks there have been always either two or four or six. I have seen two of these roosting for the night in a large sweeping thorn-tree night after night, two in a spruce fir near, and two in the ivy. The last two weeks, or since the weather became very cold, they have quartered themselves for the night mainly in the ivy. They sit on the chimneys or the pinnacles of the house for half an hour or more before bedtime, and converse, cheerfully and musically always, and sometimes mocking-bird like. But that is the more usual practice of the springtime of the year. But they are always separable into twos, only greatly more then than now.

Another craze of the fancy ornithologist, with the starling for its object, is occupying some pages of the *Naturalist* at the time of writing, the question being, 'Is the starling double-brooded?' or, in other words, 'Does the starling bring off two broods in the same season?' The question, on the face of it, is nonsensical; for it does not appear that any one of those who write on the affirmative side is willing to display so much of a crack, rather than a craze merely, as to advance that the rule with the starling is to produce two broods annually unless exceptionally prevented: and as certainly no one of those writing on the negative side disputes the fact that in divers instances they have been known to multiply to that extent.

Now for a parallel case. Some thirty years ago, or nearly, Whit-monday here signalized itself not only by the blowing of a great wind (which levelled the section that was left of my haystack), but by the falling of about three inches of snow, and two nights – those preceding and succeeding it – of very hard frost. One of the consequences was the bursting, under the tender mercies of the frosty temperature, of hosts of the grouse eggs on Westerdale moors and the equally exposed parts of our Danby high moors. The birds, however (in the majority, as I was led to think), nested again; and the consequence was that the proportion of 'cheepers' upon the moor was so great, that the practical effect was the postponing of 'The Twelfth' for a fortnight or three weeks. My impression was that perhaps one-third, or nearly so, of the broods on our high moors that year were hatched from a second laying of eggs. Yet surely no one would think, from any number of such instances of this – and they are by no means few – of styling the grouse, in the language of the *Naturalist*, double-brooded.

But even under more ordinary circumstances I could adduce similar instances from observation of the 'ways and the tricks' of the part-ridge, the ringdove, the waterhen, the dabchick, and divers other birds.

Rob them, by whatever means, of their first laying of eggs sufficiently early, or let them get off their first brood unusually soon, and they are likely to lay again and hatch the second clutch of eggs. And with the blackbird, the thrush, the robin, the chaffinch, and a score or two more of our most familiar birds, this happens in numberless instances almost every year; actually every year, I do not doubt. As to the robin, I positively knew one case in which the same pair of birds built three nests in contact with each other – like three tenements under one roof – and brought off three broods, one from each nest, in quick succession.

I mentioned the missel-thrushes as occasional plunderers. One year, why or wherefore I never could understand, they were very troublesome. They came in a flock of thirty and upwards, and always settled among the raspberry canes. If I shot at them – though I hardly succeeded in stopping more than about two in all, they were so very wary – they were back again in half an hour, and circling once or twice high up in the air, as if to see whether the coast were clear, down they swooped upon the unlucky raspberries. This was the only instance of their coming in a flight. Odd birds, or two or three at a time, I see not infrequently.

But the moor blackbird or ring-ousel is the bird of all birds to 'walk into' your fruit of the berry sort. I do not know for certain that birds do blush, or else I should say he is the most unblushing, the most unabashed of all possible delinquents in the fruit-stealing and wasting line. His effrontery exceeds that of the Irish member of fiction, of caricature even. The blackbird flies away when caught in the act with a startled cackle; the thrush retires with an apologetic cheep. But the moor blackbird – always a past master in birds' Billingsgate – swears at you, calls you all the choicest names in his repertory, blackguards you for interfering with his meal, and if forced to make himself scarce, does so with the assurance emphatically delivered and repeated that 'you are no gentleman'. I have sometimes ventured to represent to them that I thought I had a little right in my own garden, even if it was only to see what sort of a feed they were getting. They flatly and insultingly declined to see it. I suppose it must have been the rankling of their contumelious treatment of me which always made me gloat with a fine sense of compensation obtained, whenever one of them fell a victim to my avenging gun.

Some years large numbers of these birds are produced on our moors. Sometimes I have seen them, when out with my gun, well on into

September, in flocks of some hundreds together. This would be of course at the commencing stage of their making ready to 'flit' at the accustomed 'term'. If it so happens that there is a plentiful harvest of bilberries, it is very seldom we see them in the gardens very early. Nay, even our common blackbirds go up on to the moors to share in the feast, when it so befalls. During this past autumn I have seen the plainest evidences that foraging parties of blackbirds had gone from the very centre of the dale, and had not come away empty. If any one suggests that there is no reason why blackbirds, and thrushes too, should not have an occasional picnic on the moors as well as what the Suffolk people used to call 'humans', I have nothing to say against it, except that I think they must picnic every day of the week, for ten or fifteen days together.

When the bilberries are exhausted, then down come the moor blackbirds; and if they are let alone, they show that bilberries are better appetizers than sherry-bitters, or even than the boasted solan. I have literally seen them fifty at a time in this garden, on occasions when they had been left undisturbed for two or three days. It is then that they resent so bitterly and so abusively your intrusion upon their refreshment-room. After the somewhat precarious time in the gardens is over, and that much-grudged supply is exhausted, they fall back upon the berries of the mountain-ash or rowan-tree, and as these trees are fairly abundant throughout the district, there is usually a fair board spread for their enjoyment during the greater part of the period they have yet to spend in the haunts of their callow-hood. And after that comes departure.

Certainly I should be quite willing to have my mountain-ash berries spared, and it is a little trial to me to see their beauty destroyed in the shamelessly wasteful, extravagant manner in which these marauders deal with them. They begin before they are quite red-ripe, and for one they eat out of the gorgeous clusters, they seem to squander three, and drop them recklessly to cumber the paths and beds beneath. But that is the character of all the plundering perpetrated by these members of the Thrush family. They run their bill through the ripened or ripening side of a big strawberry – big enough to furnish such a bird a full meal for the time – and then pass on and do the same by another and another, wasting at least twice as many as they consume. It is only among the smaller varieties of the strawberry that I ever find a hull from which all the berry has been cleanly cleared away. It is the same with the currants, the gooseberries, the raspberries. Your red currants and your black currants spot the ground beneath the bushes with brilliantly translucent coral and lustrous beads of jet; but they are beads that will never be strung or gladden a creature's eye. The poor gooseberries too, their skins hang half empty on the bushes and rot; and the raspberries droop in raggedly granulated halves, or stick in dismembered grains on the leaves or ground below.

Woodpeckers were anything but uncommon here till lately, but what with cutting the wood down and what with shooting the occasional visitors, the visits of these harmless, interesting, beautiful birds are strangely like those of angels. I wish our bird-murderers had as much sense as Balaam's ass, and could recognize the angel of kindness to living creatures when she steps in between them and their intended victim.

The raven has been extirpated within my time. The barn owl – they used to breed in the church-tower – had gone a few years before. The brown owl, wood owl, or screech owl, if it exists still, is represented by one pair only; and I used to know of two nests in the Park[1] alone, and there were other two or three pairs about the woods near the lodge, and again others in the Crag Wood; and any still evening one could hear their note in two or three different directions. But now it is seldom indeed that I hear the – to me, as well as to Gilbert White – musical hoot of the owl of the woods.

The beautiful merlins, too, are comparatively little seen, and their place almost knoweth them no more. For they had a place since I have been here. There was a moorland point no great way from the so-called British village on Danby Low Moors where they bred regularly – at least, nested; for their eggs seldom escaped the gamekeeper or his watchers. Indeed, there were often two pairs on that part of the moors; and in days yet older they were not infrequently found haunting the high moors. And I have not seen a harrier or a buzzard these thirty years. Last year a sparrowhawk dashed into a spreading thorn-tree

[1] The Park is the name of one of the two bits of old woodland till recently left in the parish; but the wood in it now is no longer old wood. All the old trees have been cut down within the last twenty-five years, and the ground replanted with spruce, larch, and Scotch pine. The imposing-looking name is due to the circumstance that it was a part of the 'park and warren' granted by the king to the old Brus barons. It was of great extent; for, beginning at a point westward of the site of the Brus stronghold, it extended to below Lealholm Bridge, as is abundantly testified (if need were) by the many local names along its length still embodying the element 'park', as Park-end, Park-nook, Park-house, Underpark, etc.

which shelters part of my lawn, sweeping very near me as he did so; and he took his sparrow from a chattering, squabbling group, who, if they had not been so loud and spiteful in their mutual recriminations, might not have attracted the hawk, or been so unluckily blind to his proximity. But the hawk of all others I miss the most is that bird of graceful flight, and almost gracefuller poising and balancing, the kestrel or windhover. The 'little red hawk', they used to call him here, as they called the merlin the 'little blue hawk'. But alas for the poor kestrel! Among the most useful and quite the least harmful of predaceous birds, the beings whose 'eyes have not been opened' either by angels or otherwise, have given him a bad name, and plundered and shot him and his too nearly to the verge of extermination.

All the same the kestrels are ridded out of the country; and so are the weasels, as well as the owls. And what is the consequence, or one of the consequences?

An inordinate increase of field mice, long tails and short tails, and all sorts of tails together. It is a fact that my gardener killed down the mice in and about this garden last year to such an extent that he thought there was not another left anywhere near. It is a further fact that, our first snow falling on 27th November, the official just named saw that he must set his traps, and sunken pankins of water, and other mouse-catching enginery at work, and within the eighteen days which have passed since then he has caught thirty-five mice – mostly long tails – in the garden. And only yesterday our principal farmer said to me, 'The mole-catcher keeps down the moudiewarps all right; but we shall have to have somebody to look after thae mice. They're getting to be over bad for owght with the holes they mak's in the fields, and the heaps of earth they brings out.' And this was *apropros* to my complaint that they had got into the church – not a house near it anywhere – and had injured our valuable American organ to such an extent that it would cost several pounds to make the damage good. They have actually eaten some of the wooden stop-couplers quite through.

But to return to our birds. I have twice seen the great gray shrike; one a fine mandarin drake has appeared in the beck – an escaped bird from some aviary, of course. Once during a walk by the beck-side I saw a goosander – either a hen or a young bird of the year; for it was in the so-called 'dundiver' plumage – and an interchange of attention passed between us. It came up from a fishing-dive close to the bank on which I was walking – so close to me that barely four feet of space intervened between me and it. Luckily I saw it before it saw me; and there might be a reason for that; for it had something else to attract, and, indeed, occupy its attention. I said it had come up from a fishing-dive, and it had the prey it had captured all alive and kicking between its serrated mandibles, and as the said prey – a nice little trout of about six inches long – lay crosswise of the bill, the wagglings and quiverings of the fish affected the bird in some degree. But whether the fact that I saw the bird before the bird saw me might thus be accounted for or not, the result was that I had time to pull up short and stiffen myself as rigidly as I could. And there we remained for, I should say, a hundred seconds, the bird watching me and I watching the bird. I knew it would dive like a flash if I moved a finger and I constrained myself to be still. At the end of the said seconds the diving-duck brought his trout adroitly and quickly round – too quickly for me to see how it was done – so that its head was in the gape and the tail outside ready to follow. And follow it did. In a moment where there had been a trout there was a straight vacuum, and the next instant the sundiver was in flight.

On similar walks I have seen a golden-eye, not in full plumage; and a good specimen of the tufted duck; and my eldest boy one day got an immature red-necked grebe. This was a rare bird indeed; and Graham, the bird-stuffer at York, told me it was but the fourth he had seen in forty years' experience.

Once, and only once, I have seen a little grebe or dabchick in our stream; but two or three times I have come upon the water-rail. One I shot as it ran along the nearly dry bottom of a deep ditch with sufficiently steep banks, thinking it was a rat; for the movements of this bird, as well as of its congener the landrail, are of an even, non-undulating, gliding character, not what we usually understand by the word 'running'. See the awkward, grotesque action of the Cochin-China fowl, with its long ungainly legs, or of a full-grown turkey, and compare them with the rapid, even running of the partridge or grouse, and you have the very sublimity of absurdly awkward action and movement suggested and illustrated. But even the partridge, as compared with the rails, runs much as the old cow does as contrasted with the graceful tripping of the milkmaid the poet's eye is able to behold.

Another day I was sitting on the bank of the beck at a point where the current widens out into a good sheet, after having come rollicking down a series of sharp streams, and as if pausing to take breath before going a header over a sharper descent still, with a narrower course, and a bottom rockily uneven enough to insist upon a good deal of acrobatic motion on the part of the stream. As I sat, perfectly still, with a high bank opposite to me sloping up to the grass field above, and more or less overgrown with whins (many of which, however, had been burnt and stubbed not so long before), all at once a water-rail came in view, perfectly at home and entirely unconcerned, and gave me a glimpse of the ways and manners and tricks of the bird in its private life. It glided in and out among the coarse and somewhat sparse herbage, never pecking, as other birds do, on or about the ground, but evidently on the look-out for its own peculiar class of 'grub', and finding it where such classes of food are to be found, viz. sticking to the stems of grasses or other coarse vegetation capable of supporting the weight of a small snail shell with its occupant inside. It flirted its tail now and then, when it made a rather longer glide or twist than usual, much after the fashion of the water-hen; and it was curious indeed to note how it steered itself among the intricacies and obstacles besetting its path. I was able to observe all its actions, gestures, movements, captures (as it appeared), for a space of ten to fifteen minutes, when something or other disturbed it, and in a moment it was gone.

Indeed, the ease and rapidity with which these birds – both the landrail and the water-rail – move amid the obstacles apparently presented by the thick growth of herbage, whether in a corn-field, or in a clover-field or meadow, is a matter I have seen adverted to in many different notices of the habits or peculiarities of the genus by divers writers on natural history topics. Yarrell, I think it is, who suggests that the bird is specially framed for such a purpose, having what he calls 'a compressed form of body'. It is perfectly true; and equally true that both birds trust, and with good reason, to the expedient of flight on foot in preference to that of flight on the wing. It is almost impossible to flush a rail a second time, even if the dog be put on the track almost immediately after the bird has reached the covert.

One day, some twenty or twenty-five years ago, I had arranged with one of the principal yeomen here to go with him to Glaisdale Swangs – a wet, morassy division of the Danby and Glaisdale high moors – our object being to get, if we could, a few couples of golden plover. I had for long practised the imitation of the cry uttered by the golden plover, especially when they are on the ground; and I flattered myself I could do it rather well – as, indeed, I think I could. Our plan was to

walk towards and over the likely haunts, and get a shot or two before
the birds became restless, as they do when disturbed by intrusion into
the haunts which are usually, after the height of the grouse-shooting,
but little interfered with either by shepherd or dog. The moor thereabouts is too wet to be so much affected by the moor-sheep as other
parts are. We got two or three shots in this way, and then we separated
to take our own private chances of a passing flight or a few stray
birds still about the ground, and either stalking or calling any of whose
comparative vicinity we might become aware. I do not think either of
us was remarkably successful for a full hour after we had separated, and
I was beginning to think our bag would be light. Suddenly I heard the
call of a plover, and under what seemed to be the most favourable circumstances. The moor rose from where I was standing with a gradual
slope, but little broken for the third part of a mile or more, and the call
came from the upper part of the ridge, but quite evidently from some
little distance on the other side of it. I replied to the call, and to my
delight there was an almost immediate answer. A minute or so elapsed,
during which I was cautiously approaching the point from over which
the cry seemed to come, and I called again. Another response, and
evidently the bird had been drawing nearer to me as I had been drawing
nearer to it. The same interchange of call and reply continued at the
intervals of a half-minute or so, and for a sufficiently long space to
allow me to have got to within forty or fifty yards of the ridge. I was
crouching as low as possible all the latter part of the ascent, and I made
sure that, on rising from my stooping attitude and making a quick rush
to the ridge, I should have a shot within very easy distance. The call
from the other side came just then, and my reply was the best spurt I
could make with my gun at the ready. I had not covered two yards
when I saw my companion's hat, and a second later his gun, at the ready
also. He had been answering my calls as regularly as I addressed them
to the supposed plover. I hardly need say that the only explosion which
took place was a united one of rather shamefaced but very hearty laugh-
ter at our mutual discomfiture.

Thirty or forty years ago I could see three or four pairs of the dipper
any day I walked by the beck-side, or rambled up the course of one of
our brattling moor streams on their downward run to help the volume
of what we call, by way of distinction, 'the big beck'. But now, where
I used to see six or eight or perhaps ten pairs, I barely see one. I wish I
had a fairy godmother, and that fairy godmothers were as potent as in

Cinderella times! The favour I would try my most ingratiating ways to obtain should be – nothing truculent or bloodthirsty, although I do not love the reckless shooters of rock-birds, rare birds, swallows for practice, pigeons at blackguard pot-shop matches, *et hoc genus omne* – but that every gun-carrying lout who wantonly shot a poor harmless bird of any kind whatever without a cause, should be sentenced – not to judicial or other blindness, but – to inability to hit his mark again for ever and a day. What earthly good or satisfaction there can be in shooting a dipper I cannot conceive; and yet they have been thinned in the way I have mentioned. In the loneliest walk they are always companions and always cheerful besides. To see him come out of the water as if on purpose to say, 'Good morning to you! Isn't it a nice cheery morning? Oh, it's so jolly,' and then to hear him sing his cheery little song, standing on a stone just awash in the bed of the stream; and then to see him, with something very like a nod and a wink with his bright eye, just trip into the water and go tumbling and toddling along the bottom for half a score yards – why, it is as good as killing a couple of snipe, right and left, to an embryo sportsman.

I have come across their nests now and again in the district around. One of the small tributary becks running down this dale proceeds by Ainthorpe, passing through a spacious garden by aid of a capacious culvert; then comes into the open air again in a wild little griff; then is culverted over again; and when it emerges it is just bursting into the road to the Station, but after a leap of a yard or so, is caught in the open mouth of another culvert, down which it slips abashed right underneath the roadway. Just within the rude arch of this culvert a pair of dippers bred for some years. But one unlucky day some of the boys from the school, intent on getting their feet wet, or some like piece of schoolboy self-indulgence, found it; and the haunt once known, there was no future peace for the poor dippers. Another nest I knew was in a hole in one of the piers of a bridge guiltless of arches, lying on the road from Danby End to Castleton. A couple of young fellows then living in my house were fishing one day close to this bridge, when a very heavy thunder shower came on; and for shelter, their feet and legs being already wet with wading, they resorted to the landward arch-space (as it should have been), and so were in a position to see the ingress of a dark bird which flew straight to a put-log hole; just above their reach as they stood, but which they managed to explore nevertheless; finding therein a dipper's nest, and in it well on to half a dozen white eggs.

CHAPTER TEN

Winter on the Moors

Yes, I have seen some winter weather in this out-of-the-way place. I have seen the snow gathered in drifts of fifteen, eighteen, twenty feet in thickness; I have seen it gathering, piling itself up in fantastic wreaths, sometimes busy only in accumulating substance and solidity, like a yeoman of the elder days, and gathering at the rate of six feet or seven feet in thickness in from twelve hours to twenty-four. And once I saw it gathering – and gathering a foot deep in the hour, moreover – before ever a flake of new snow had fallen, and when the old snow was caked over with a crisp crust, the result of diurnal or sun-thaws and nocturnal freezings again. And the manner of it was on this wise.

It had been a fine day till past twelve o'clock, and it seemed good for walking. There was a young farmer in the parish, at the very eastern boundary of it, distant four miles and a half of good walking the way I had to take, whom I wanted to see. Besides being the son of one of the oldest and staunchest friends I had in the parish – the old gamekeeper, in point of fact – he was in great trouble. He had been engaged to a young woman, also belonging to the parish, for a number of years; the banns had been asked out, and the wedding-day was fixed. On that very day I had to bury her. She had been seized with illness while ordering some of the wedding gear, and died in two or three hours. And I wanted to go and see him, and talk to him a little. My walk to his place was accomplished without difficulty; pleasantly indeed, as far as roads and weather were concerned. But I had noticed before I had reached my limit in that direction that the day, and the weather most likely, were going to change; and so I was not surprised on setting my face southwards, instead of westwards and homewards, to find that the wind was rising, and rising sharply, not to say fiercely. But I wanted to see another parishioner, the widow of another old and staunch parochial friend, who had been ailing lately, and so I persevered with the extension of my walk. This led me into Fryup Head, the house I sought being well on to three miles from the house I left. It was still perfectly fair overhead, the sun shining brightly at times; and the snow – no great thickness of it anywhere; perhaps two or three inches where it was thickest – was crusted over, as I said. But the wind grew colder and colder as it increased momentarily in force; and long before I got to my widowed parishioner's house the crusted snow had begun to be broken up by the force of the wind, and to drive along in most incisive fragments. There were already, when I got to within a field or two of the house, drifts formed in parts of the road approaching it such that the wheels of a recently-passing vehicle had cut through some of them to the depth of eighteen inches. Almost my first remark on entering the house was to the daughter, of whom I asked if the wheel-tracks I had noted were made by any trap driven by a member of the family, hoping that, if so, he would not be long away, or else he 'would be matched to get home again; for it was safe there was going to be a "hap" '. I did not prolong my visit, for things were looking badly for my walk home – a more than four miles' walk the nearest way I could go, and that way from corner to corner of fields, over the loose stone-walls; and real rough walking.

It was quite time I was afoot. Some idea may be formed of the fury of the wind from the fact that, as I paused at the corner of the second field, up which the drift of the snowcrust had pursued me with cutting sharpness – the pause being due to the strong necessity of making my way safely over a broken wall with a deep drop on the other side – the sharp-edged particles driven with the full force of the wind against the nape of my neck and the more exposed ear and cheek, inflicted such acute pain that it required some nerve to bear it and keep busy with getting over the nasty, dangerous place. Once over, the worst was also over. There were still two more walls to surmount, but then downhill, across a sloping field, and into the road again. My way lay, for the most part, for a mile under the lee of a five-foot wall, and I got along well. But when I came to the gateways through the wall there were snow-banks across the road and a thick stifling drift of sharp snow-powder to work through, as well as the loose snow about my feet and legs. I met one of our farmers on horseback, who could scarcely speak so as to be heard for the blast and the powdery snow. But I managed to hear part of his greeting as we met and passed. 'It's a savage day, mister', was all I heard, and I echoed his sentiment. On reaching the castle the direction of my march altered, and I had the wind behind me. But there was a difficulty at the first gate across the road I came to.

There was a drift just through it, nearly four feet thick, and it reached several yards along the road. And I have known things easier of going than plunging through three or four feet of utterly loose snow.

All this time not a flake of fresh or soft snow had fallen. It was perfectly fair overhead, though thickening up from half-hour to half-hour with a prophetic intimation of what was yet to come. And come it did, though not for two or three hours after I reached home, and had at last got the snow out of my hair and beard.

All that night it snowed, and the next day. I wanted to go to the station and the post on the first of the two days, and the roads were known to be so full, and the drift was so very bad, that my people would not let me go alone; so my gardener and eldest lad at home – the latter for the fun of it – went with me. Within a quarter of a mile of the parsonage I found snow in the road over seven feet thick in one place; and, for scores of yards together, my track lay along a snow-covered fence – above it, not by the side of it. The next day the seven feet of snow in the road had become fourteen, and there was not a place in the entire road for the distance of six or seven hundred yards where the snow lay less deep than five feet, and in places it was from eight to ten. To get along at all, we broke the fences and plunged along the fields parallel with the line of road.

These accumulations in the roads, however, are all in the way of business, and we are used to them. But the pranks played by the snow at times would be amusing, even interesting, if they were not so baffling and tiresome. A great wind, with snow dry enough to drift, either already on the ground or still falling, or, as likely as not, both together, catches hold of the snow as it sweeps over these lofty moorland ridges and drives it irresistibly before it until it loses its grip; and that is when the force of gravity becomes greater than the force of propulsion; and this happens on the lee side of a wall, and *a fortiori*, on the lee side of one of these mountainous moorland ridges. But the snow has this curious circumstance attending it, that it does not fall perpendicularly on reaching the sheltered part; on the contrary, it seems to become slightly cohesive, and begins to form a projecting ledge from the edge of the sheltering object. I have watched the process on the sheltered side of a seven-foot wall, the top of which was almost level with the face of the land on the other side of it. First the level was attained by the lodgment of snow above the wall. Then the ledge began to form, slightly curvilinear in section; the ledge itself being, so to speak, undercut like a volute in sculpture. Below, on the sheltered side, there is always a sort of gentle undercurrent of air, the action of which is to keep the foot of the wall – if it be a wall we are watching – free from any accumulation of snow for a foot or two away from it, according to height; but also to blow the falling particles upwards against the under side of the growing ledge, which is thus thickened both from above and below, as well as helped to grow in the direction of its projection. One Sunday morning as I was going to my service at Fryup I noted all this going on at one particular place, almost devised on purpose to permit observation of the process, and I took my notes with some nicety. I returned the same way something under two hours later, and found that the ledge had advanced about six inches, and grown in proportional thickness as well; as, perhaps, goes without saying.

This was on the road-side of a stone wall nearly seven feet high. As I stood face to face with it and watched it, on my left, sloping upwards from my very feet, for upwards of one hundred and twenty yards of actual altitude – and the last twenty yards very steeply – was the flank of one of our moory ridges, and I have once and again seen the ledge of snow I have been trying to describe project from the edge or brae of the ridge from sixteen or twenty feet to sixteen or twenty yards. Once, in going to my afternoon service on foot – I could not have gone half a mile either on wheels or horseback, as the roads were all full – on reaching the brae at the point where my ordinary track begins to descend, I found a snow precipice of sixteen feet deep, apparently cutting off all further progress. But there was a projecting ledge of snow about a foot in width some ten feet below the upper edge, and I thought I could let myself drop or slide down to that, and bring myself up there. The plan was successful. But on considering my landmarks on reaching the foot of this wall of snow, I found the edge I had dropped from was at least eighteen to twenty yards in advance of the edge of the brae.

There were thirteen of my Fryup parishioners gathered for the service at the foot of the slope, watching my proceedings. The greater part of these inclined to think I would not attempt the descent. Those who had known me longest said, 'T' priest wadn't be bett.' And the event justified their confidence. But the service over, there arose the question of how I was to get back again; and when I said, 'The same way as I came,' one oldish man besought me not to attempt it; 'it was over parlous for owght.' Nay, he was so urgent that he actually shed tears over my foolhardiness, as he considered it. However, I was not to be dissuaded, and though it was a 'parlous' thing in a way, it was safely accomplished. One of my boys, a lad of about sixteen, was with me, and one of us had a strong stick and the other an equally strong umbrella. These I stuck firmly into the snow wall, the one a foot higher than the other, and then working holes in with my feet until I succeeded in getting foothold, I was able to move one of my two handholds a foot higher, and to get a higher foothold; and so on alternately, until at last, after great labour and much delay, I succeeded in reaching the top. But had it not been for the sort of channel worked into the snow by our downward slide I do not think it could have been done.

But the most laborious, and perhaps the most venturesome, snow walk I ever had was from Easington to Danby. I had exchanged duties with my oldest clerical friend and neighbour, George Morehead, Rector of Easington, with the understanding that, while he returned to Easington, the three duties done, I, after my three at Easington and Liverton, should stay all night at the rectory, and have my trap sent over for me in the morning. There had been a slight shower of snow while the Liverton service was going on, but hardly enough to do more than whiten the ground; and when I had finished the evening duty at Easington, it was a beautiful starlight night, and no one had thought of, much less expected, a fall of snow. But on looking out at eight in the morning, to my intense surprise, there was a dense covering of white over all. It soon became apparent from the reports brought in that the passage of wheels along the level would be intensely difficult, and over such hills and moor-roads as lay between Easington and Danby simply impossible. I was most anxious to get home for different reasons; and, resisting the more than urgent entreaties of my dear old friend and his wife, I determined to set forth on foot. For the first three to four miles the walking, though very fatiguing – for there was not an inch of the way with less than a foot deep of the yielding snow, which permitted no firm foothold among it – was practicable enough. As I passed Sir Charles (then Mr) Palmer's lodge-gates at Grinkle I ascertained that, there being somewhat urgent need to send a carriage to Danby Station, the road had been explored to see if by dint of sending on the snow-plough a passage could be effected; but the attempt had been given up as hopeless. However, I determined to persevere, and reached the purely moor part of the trudge at Waupley. Here the difficulties began in good earnest. Though there had been no drifting in the sheltered road, yet on reaching the open moor it proved to be very different; for every

few yards drifts of from two to four feet deep intervened, and continued to intervene. However, I struggled on until I reached the highest
level I had to cross over, and it was a dreary scene before me indeed!

I had already been a little impressed with the utter isolation of my
walk. All life, even bird life, seemed to have disappeared. I knew the
moors had hundreds of grouse on them. I never saw one nor heard one.
I had seen two blackbirds when making my way along a part of the
road which was also for two or three score yards the course of a small
stream; and, strange to say, I had seen a goldfinch – the only one I have
ever seen in this district – just after reaching the moor at Waupley.
Besides these 'feathered fowl' I saw only two or three moor pipits,
usually numerous enough on the moors at all times of the year. I
hardly wondered at this scarcity of bird life, for it was a cruel day. The
intensity of the cold may be estimated by this – that as I walked and
labouringly perspired (I was in fact so wet that I literally had not a
'dry thread' about me) – the perspiration settled and froze on my eye-
brows and hair, and freezing into little balls tinkled against the steel of
my spectacles more musically than pleasantly; and naturally the birds
and all the other creatures dwelling on or about the moors would be
seeking such shelter as could be found or made available. I did not even
see or hear a single moor sheep.

On reaching a given point on the level aforesaid, where a cross-track
deflected from the course of the high road in such a way as to cut off an
angle and save a distance of nearly half a mile, feeling the temptation to
try and save so much of the trying fag I was experiencing, I attempted
to take the said short cut. The snow looked level enough, but I had
not allowed for the unevennesses and hollows of the moor concealed
beneath the fair-seeming surface, and before I had waded five-and-
twenty yards from the line of the road I found myself struggling to
get out of a dish-like hollow in which the snow was deep enough to
reach above my waist, and deepening every foot I advanced. Clearly
the 'short cut' would be no saving, and I struggled back as well as I
could to regain the line of the road. I had almost begun to despair of
getting through with my walk, when I saw a moving object coming over
the top of the ridge next to that on which my path lay; and I presently
saw that it was a cart with two horses in it, and two men in attendance
on them. This gave me renewed hope, not to say confidence, for they
were coming the very way I had to go, and of course they must have
tracked the road for me. At the rate of our relative progress it took a

long time to cross the intervening space, but at last we met. They were Liverton men who had been under the extremest necessity for want of fuel, and they had been literally forced to make the effort to get to Danby Station for a load of coal. The snow was now drifting freely, and the travelling was momentarily becoming worse; but even when they had started they had provided against the emergencies they foresaw by putting two horses to their cart, doubling also the ordinary force of men – two instead of one only – and providing themselves with shovels to clear their way if necessary, or dig their 'draught' out, if need arose. All the load they had ventured to lay on with all their appliances had been six hundredweight, and only yesterday (4th December 1889) I met a man who had travelled the same road with a load of coal in a waggon drawn by three horses, who had then, as he told me, well on to two tons weight, easily drawn by his team. And the two men I met that day had to walk, partly because their horses were barely able to drag the cart with its light load without their weight added, and partly because the foremost had to guide the leader over the trackless white waste (with only a bit of ling growing on the braes on either side of the moor road to show here and there where it actually was), as well as help it in its plunging efforts to get through the deeper places; and the other with the shaft horse to keep it steady to its work. They both of them knew me, and were simply astounded to see me there on foot alone and under such circumstances and surroundings.

For the first half-mile after meeting them I found the track they had made of the greatest service to me; although every step I took was through snow that reached above my knees; and, even before I reached the top of the ridge on which I had first caught sight of them, the said track was being rapidly obscured by the drifting in upon it of fresh snow. On the other side of the ridge the track was gone in places; but it was practically downhill now, the most part of the way, and my worst difficulties things of the past; and I reached home safe, wretchedly wet, and more exhausted than I knew, or had allowed for.

The snow came on again before long, and before the week was out enough had fallen to make an even covering all over the face of the country of about twenty-seven inches thick. The Sunday following was without any further fall, and it was possible to get to my more distant chapel; but the man who drove me, and who had driven me, as he expressed it, thousands of miles – he was the Daniel of my houe-digging experiences – declared (and still declares) he had never had such a journey before. It was indeed, from the difficulties of the roadway alone, an awful drive. I think the fatigue in another way was as bad as that of the plunging, struggling tramp from Easington to Danby. And the next day I was in bed, very seriously ill. My medical attendant shook his head over me, and said he must see me again the next day – he had ten miles to ride to get here – and when he came shook his head more gravely still. 'He would come again as early the following day as he could!' But he did not come. Another fall of snow made the journey from Guisborough here impracticable alike by road and by rail; and for six days I lay hovering between life and death, and the doctor not able to get near me!

That is one of my reminiscences of a moorland parish in the winter-time. I think it was the worst winter I have known here. The cross-road which runs east and west past the school, about a quarter of a mile north of the parsonage, was so full up with hardened, beaten-down snow, that one of my sons as he walked along it was able to pluck twigs off the road-side trees, which were high enough to admit of the passage beneath them of the mighty loads of corn or hay as they are piled up in order to be taken out of the fields into the stack-garth.

Probably it will be anticipated by those who have read the preceding pages that on our wide, wild, shelterless moors here, even the Suffield Heights accumulation might be, or would be, outdone. And indeed it was. A little below the top of Gerrick Bank, on the highroad from Whitby to Guisborough, and on the side nearer to the last named place, the snow was deep enough and compact enough to admit of being tunnelled through, so as to admit of the passage of the coach working between the two places; and the tunnel stood for more than a week.

On our Danby moors, at a place about two miles distant from the point named as Gerrick Bank-top, there is a narrow gully or rift, with steeply sloping sides, ling covered, ascending to a height of about a hundred feet perpendicularly above the level of the trickling moor-stream running through the gully below. This was filled from bottom to top, so that there was an even slope from the slightly higher brae on the west to the lower one on the other side. And the old gamekeeper, who was the first to tell me of the incident, added that a very dry spring and early summer succeeded, and the moors became so dry that the moor-birds had to travel considerable distances to get to water, and that he had seen them come in scores to drink of the water which trickled from the melting snow as late as Midsummer day.

But the most extraordinary feat I have ever known as achieved in the way of the making of snowdrifts by our moorland blasts, took place during the winter of 1886–87, and the account of it was given me by the 'gaffer' of the small band of road-minders and menders employed by the township. The wind had blown from the north and east when the snow began to be derivable, and he had had some difficulty in keeping the door of his own dwelling, a house on the very edge of the moor, three-quarters of a mile from the site of my own, clear, and one night he had taken the precaution to carry his shovel indoors, with the almost certainty that he would have to dig his way out in the morning; inasmuch as the passage he had cut and kept clear from day to day was filling fast at the darkening, and there was every appearance of a terrible night of snow and drifting. Armed with his well-brightened tool – for he had been snow-cutting for days whenever there seemed a chance of doing it to any effect – he opened his door in the early light, and strange, incredible as it seemed, there was no big wreath of snow there – no wreath at all worth thinking of. But at the other end of the house there was a gigantic accumulation piled up, and reaching almost to the gable point of the roof. The wind had shifted during the night and had transported the results of its action during the previous days from the one end to the other! And exactly the same thing had happened at the farmhouse some 200 yards more to the north, and similarly situated. My friend, the road-surveyor, was not the only one among us who went to bed with a shovel – not exactly under his pillow, but – laid quite handy for use the first thing in the morning; and who had to use it too. At the public-house on the hill opposite my house, and about half a mile distant, the oldish man who lived there and, in a sort, served the landlady, told me his first work in the morning for more than a week, after making on the fire and so forth, was to dig a way out, and both in front of the house and in its rear; and that 'mostlings it teuk a lot o' deeing'.

Late in the winter of the year before last there were five Sundays in succession during which access to the parish church was like matrimony – not to be 'lightly enterprised or taken in hand'. The first of these Sundays I had with some difficulty made my advance about half-way to the church when I met the parish-clerk, who had come forward to tell me there was but one lad at the church, and he thought it a chance if any one else either would or could come. It was a wild day indeed, the snow stouring in blinding clouds; and I thought Peter might be right, and so I turned back, meeting the wind now. It seemed absurd to say so, but it was all I could do to keep myself straight with the aid of the low hedges on either side. But for the hedges I was only too well aware I must have gone hopelessly wrong in the third of a mile between the place where Peter met me and my home.

As it happened, two men turned up at the church after Peter met me. On the next Sunday the same two men and the boy were there to meet me. On the third Sunday the same trio and a young woman. One of the men had chivalrously essayed to carry the girl over the worst of the snowdrifts, and the treacherous crust had given way beneath the united weights, and a comforting and edifying roll in the snow had been the result. I saw the parties 'laughing consumedly' as they came round the corner of the chancel, and I am afraid I laughed myself when I was told, in answer to my query, what had taken place. The fourth and fifth Sundays saw my two male friends already named, the boy, and two other men, present at the service. But all this time I could not get to my distant church in Fryup.

It would be easy enough to multiply experiences as to the difficulty, and at times the absolute impracticability, of any locomotion, either by parson or people, in respect of going to or from church, during what are in the vernacular called 'ho'ding storms'. I will but give an illustration or two, and then pass on to another topic. This house is, I suppose, some 1600 yards distant from the church—not quite a mile, but approaching to it. Two winters ago, and as late as the month of March, the drifting of the snow, under the violence of a wind blowing more from the north, had been so great that, of the said distance of nearly a mile, there were about fifty yards just near my garden, and fifty yards about half-way between this house and the church, not so snow-blocked as to forbid me to walk along the road. All the rest — say 1500 yards and more — was covered with snow to the depth of three or four feet and upwards — in most parts, six feet — and for the whole width of one field from eight up to twelve feet. Fifty yards away from my garden gate I had to break through the fence on my right hand, and make my way parallel with the road along the strips of the fields which had been swept more or less bare by the wind. To accomplish this I had to make my way through two fences running at right angles to the direction of the road, then over two loose stone walls, then through (or over) another quickset hedge, the line of which I could barely distinguish for the snow piled on and over it; and so into the field adjoining the church-yard. For three weeks there was no traffic along the road. The farmers 'up the dale', who were forced to obtain access (on account of their live stock) to Danby End, the mill there, and so forth, made a track for themselves along the land in the fields alongside the road, making gaps in the stone walls named above, and some sort of a difficult passage into and along the lane past my house. All this traffic was done on horse-back. Sacks of grain to be ground, sacks of meal to be carried home, were all conveyed on horseback.

Another time, I remember, more than twenty years ago, I had myself made my way to the church by dint of breaking the fences and eschew-ing the roadway, and when I got to the church I had not the 'legal congregation'. I waited till ten minutes past church-time, and seeing no prospect of any addition to 'Dearly Beloved' the parish-clerk and another official, I set off homewards. Half-way between the church and the parsonage I saw some one leaning against the stone wall by the side of one part of the lane or road. Coming nearer, I saw it was the school-master, a tall, strong, stout man in the prime of his age and strength. I stopped to speak to him, and added it would be no use his going on; there was no congregation, and I was on my way home. Mr. G——, in a voice that was not cheerful, said it made but little difference; he was spent, and could neither go forward nor get back home again. And indeed he did look exhausted – as well he might. For he had toiled through and through the deep snow cumbering the road for more than half a mile. I had tried it, and after the experience of the first hundred yards, had given it up as hopeless, and had broken the fence as above described. This expedient had not occurred to Mr. G——, and indeed it was the first time I had adopted it so fully myself; but when I mentioned it to him, he cheered up greatly, and readily followed my lead in clam-bering over the wall I had found him leaning against, and after a struggle with the deep snow for a few yards we found ourselves getting along without very heavy toil.

As may be assumed without previous searching inquiry, when a big stalwart master and a well-hardened and fairly resolute parson encoun-tered such difficulties in the way of getting to and from church, it was fairly certain that children due at school might not find it very easy to get there. One week, when the snow covered the road to the church as above described, the attendances at the school (excluding the master's two sons) ranged thus: the first day of the week, two boys out of the average eighty; the second day, three; the third day, two; the fourth day, three; and the fifth day, four. It was almost amusing to look in, as I did every day, and see the master and his select scholars hugging the school stove in such an affectionate manner. But another time, about six years ago, one incident of this sort almost verged on the comic. I was making my way down, not without effort or difficulty, to the station and post. Between the school and the first dwelling on the road in question lay a section of highway quite sure to be filled up speedily, given adequate snow to be driven, and a wind from the north equal to doing the driving. Neither of these elements was wanting on the day in question, and within threescore yards of the school it became necessary to take to the fields, and through the stackyard of the house aforesaid. It was a fearful day, and drifting so fast that newly-made tracks were obliterated with strange speed in places. And there were such tracks before me. Passing the stacks just named, the road was less encumbered, and when I had nearly got to the viaduct over the railway by the station, I saw a figure before me struggling through a drift six feet thick on one side of the road, and about three on the other. Through this shallower part a horse had been made to force its way, and it was in the sort of squandering, sputtering track thereby made that I saw the little object in front of me. I came up with it just before the passage was accomplished, and found it was a small boy of about eight or nine years old. 'What are you doing here, such a day as this?' I asked him. 'Please, Ah's gannan yam.' 'Why, where do you live?' said I. 'Please, sir, anenst t' blacksmith's.' – 'Well, but what are you out here for?' – 'Please, sir, Ah've been te scheeal.' – 'Been to school!' I rejoined, 'Why, there'd be no one there!' – 'Please, sir, yes, sir, there was me and t' tweea teachers.' The sturdy little chap had got through all his difficulties, and was within a hundred yards or so of his parent's house; so I gave him what coppers I had in my pocket and sent him home wishing for another and like snowy day's adventure.

But it is by no means only in such ways as the foregoing that winter signalizes itself in our moorland district. Some of the optical effects produced in times of copious snow, while it is as yet unsullied, and alike unaffected by wind or sun, are of almost incredible beauty. Almost forty years ago, at such a time, a great electrical disturbance took place in the atmosphere. I avoid the use of the term thunderstorm, because it might be misleading. The thunder was very loud, and repeated in long bellowing rolls, and the lightning was, I think, as startlingly brilliant as I have ever seen it – two occasions only excepted. But there was no downfall: neither snow nor hail nor sleet accompanied the disturbance. My children were then very young, and there was some trouble among them by reason of the alarming loudness of the thunder, and my wife was with them. I was a little startled at hearing her cry to me from the nursery door to come quickly upstairs; but the explanation was that she wished me to see the lightning and note the marvellous beauty of the scene, as flash after flash lit the whole snow-covered dale before us, and its steep retaining moorbanks on either side, with an effulgence that defies description. But the dazzling, almost intolerable brightness of the lightning-lit snow – white indeed, and with a whiteness such as 'no fuller on earth can whiten' – that forced exclaiming rapture rather than quiet admiration; while it was the most marvellous succession of most marvellous tints and tones of colour which dwelt on the retina many seconds after the flash ceased its splendid being, that dwelt in the mind and imagination. The total duration of this after-vision could not have been less than sixty seconds; and as the heavenly whiteness faded it began to be replaced by the most delicate tinge of rose, deepening by distinct gradations through darker tones into steel-blue, which in its turn gave place to the customary showing of snow by night, the night being unlit by a moon.

I have witnessed this wonderful display of nature's lights and colouring three several times now, but in no case have I seen the unimaginable glory of the first display outshone. And the remembrance of it I think is indelible.

But this strangely beautiful succession of delicate rose tints and steel-blue tones of deepening intensity has been witnessed by me once and again since the night of that marvellous display; only with this difference, that the succession of shades and colours was not a succession of time, or sequence in order of progression, but simply of distance and altitude. Or to put it another way: At your feet and in the foreground your eye rested on the unsullied snow; in the mid-distance, or on the steep slopes of the ascending moor-banks, you saw the tinges and tints of the rose; and in the far distance, or above the braes of the walls of the dales, you gazed out upon the matchless blues. The colours might be fainter than as they glowed forth after the magic operation of the lightning's blaze, but they were all there; and waited there to be gazed on with a sort of reverent admiration, until the sun had sunk too low behind the western moor-bank for it to be called day any longer. The first time I saw this exhibition of nature's colouring was on Christmas eve in the year when my walk home from a fruitless visit to the church, in company with the schoolmaster, took place. It was freezing with intense sharpness, and the night was one more intensely cold than usually befalls, even high up among the moors. As it was, at this sunset my beard and moustache were frozen into one icy mass while I stood and gazed on the gorgeous panorama; and it has only been on similar occasions of very sharp frosts, with a perfectly quiescent atmosphere, that I have ever witnessed any repetition of it.

There is still, however, one phase of winter scenery which has engraved itself as deeply as any other on my recollection, and it is one I have observed under various aspects, and on divers different occasions. What I refer to are the singularly lovely creations of a rime or white frost, on the occasions on which there is so large an amount of moisture in the atmosphere as to lead to a heavy deposit.

I remember one occasion on which the deposit was so heavy that ordinary rushes became rods of more than half an inch in diameter, the merest dry bents – windlestraws, or winn'lstraes as we call them here – the thickness of a big cedar pencil, and every small twig in the hedges a bar of glittering jewellery. It was a glorious winter's day, with some three to four inches of snow on the level in the fields, and with a temperature so frosty in the morning that the moisture of my breath congealed with every expiration on the hair about my mouth and chin. On looking at any of the objects I have named with a little attention it was seen that the incrustation depended on what may – for the purposes of illustration – be described as a coating of fur, every constituent filament in which was as compound as the upper shoot and branches of a fir-tree. There was the spire on an infinitesimal scale, with the whorl of radiating spurs at its foot, and the same repeated at the foot of the second shoot of the leader, and so on. Anything more strangely, mysteriously, ethereally beautiful I never beheld. Each twig, each grassy seed-stem, each blade of grass, and especially each longer and thicker shoot or rush, was a miracle of symmetry, beauty, perfection, composite of myriads of marvels on a lessened and lessening scale.

But these wonderful creations by nature's jeweller were not limited only to the vesture of such objects as those I have named. When I went forth on my afternoon's expedition to Fryup Church – for it was on a Sunday that this fairy world of ornamentation greeted my eyes – and had made my way into a large smooth field, on pausing to look back

towards the north-west and north sides of the snow-scape, having the
brightly shining sun on my side as I did so, my eye was caught by
the myriads of glittering points that gemmed the whole surface of the
snow. The whole area for hundreds and hundreds of square yards was
lit up in this way; and there was not a hue or a lustre displayed by the
diamond that was not repeated by thousands of resplendent facets
bestrewing the field. There were simply acres of lustrous diamonds!

Naturally I turned to a closer examination of the circumstances and
conditions leading on to the marvellous scene which gladdened my
eyes; it was indeed the 'joy' of a 'thing of beauty'. And I then observed,
what my somewhat impaired sight had not suggested to me before, that
the entire surface of the snow was covered with – to use the word once
already applied in the same connection – a thick fur of sprays of frost-
work like that on the twigs and grass, only three-quarters of an inch in
the pile. Every step I had taken had crushed and destroyed myriads of
frost-gems, all symmetrically perfect and beautiful, and set as no jeweller on earth could set them. Still, though these glimmered with a sort of
pearly lustre in the sunbeams, the sources of the flashing, lustrously-
hued diamond rays were not in them; but set among them in infinite
numbers were facets of such reflecting and refracting power as only
Nature herself can produce, and set at every conceivable angle, as well
as endlessly diversified in size. I no longer wondered that the brightness and the splendour were so dazzlingly glorious to behold, when I
came to regard the enginery from which they resulted.

One other instance of filigree work of a like nature may also be
mentioned. I have seen it only during two winters, in the course of
which we had not only much snow on the ground, and very heavy
drifts of the same, but also after the drifting wind had subsided a series
of intense frosts – the thermometer down to zero, and one or two nights
three to five degrees below. If any one can imagine the filaments of a
spider's web encrusted as I have tried to describe the twigs and grass as
being, and can further try and realize them, not as in the radiations and
concentric circumferences of the great field-spider's geometrical work,
but erring and straying in all sorts of graceful and unstudied confusion
from one fold of the wreathed snow to another, some of them six or
seven inches long, and many less than half that, and all being more or
less vertical, he will have a faint idea of the decorative energies of hoar-
frost where there would seem to be no substratum of fibres for it to
work upon. This kind of work, however, was always on the wall-like

drifts on the north side of the roads, or where the sun during the short period of his winter's warmth had been exercising such softening influences as were permitted to him under such circumstances.

Once or twice also I have seen the snow in such places and with such aspect look as if, so to speak, honeycombed, but in the most delicate fashion, by the agency of the sun's rays; and then the aggregate group of tiny borings and indentations all furred at the edge and in the cavities with a cognate garniture of minute crystallizations – again one of the most beautiful vagaries of the frost-artist.

Again, the sun may 'come forth as a bridegroom out of his chamber, and rejoice as a giant to run his course', but, of a surety, this Dales country of ours with its mighty moor-banks, when draped and veiled in the marvellous garments of pure, undriven snow, may be the image of the bride ready to respond to his first smiles in the coming morning.

But similes apart, the dales are so deep, and the moor-banks are so up-sweeping when mantled with fresh and deep snow, and the snow itself is so white, that while the accustomed eye revels in the return of unforgotten beauty, and recalls with gratified recognition this or that well-known feature, the unaccustomed eye is fairly bewildered with the strange, pale beauty of the snow-scape, and for a time at least seems to be incapable of fixing on any idea save that of an immensity of whiteness. The recognition of beauty and grandeur comes later.

But indeed, it is not only in the winter time, or when the hills are snow-draped and the dales snow-clad, that the marvels of beautiful colouring are displayed for the delight of the watching eye. A hundred times, and again a hundred, I have seen in the early autumn evenings, when the sun was sinking behind the western banks, all the moorland heights towards the east and north, as they rose in their receding order, take on the most lovely and delicate hues of violet and purple, glorified with the bloom of the plum and the sheen of infinite velvet.

Once, too, in the late autumn, in the afternoon of a rayless day, I was coming from Westerdale over the end of the ridge traversed by the road from thence to Castleton, when the most amazing, unimaginable study in colour was spread out before my astonished gaze. For I had seen the moor-scape a thousand times before, and enjoyed its varied beauty, here rough and rugged and there softened and swelling with graceful undulations; but I had never dreamed of the glory it might wear when gorgeously apparalled in array of Nature's own garnishing. At my feet and in the near foreground was what, on ordinary days, we

looked upon as the ling dulled and browned by lapse and wear of the
past season; in the middle distance, and rising just beyond it, were the
valleys of the youthful Esk and the Baysdale beck, still green and
fringed with green, and backed by the strong slopes of the Crown End
and other moorland banks, all swept and charactered by broad fields
and patches of russet bracken; and in the remoter distance, just bank
behind bank rising in dim solemnity, and all clad in the dulled uniform
brown of the ling of autumn. But to-day, although the contours
remained, and with them the material features of the scenery throughout,
all else was changed. All that was everyday, commonplace, dull, was
refined, all that was worn and faded was renewed and glorified; and not
a thing left to remind us of the old, the worn, the faded, or the unbeauti-
ful. At my feet and before me was, as it were, a carpet, hundred-piled,
of the richest brown, such shades as I had never seen nor imagined;
the greens of the valleys were become the greens – and only there
seen – of the sky in a gorgeous sunset; the fields and sheets of bracken
were spaces of 'old gold' and burnished gold, and all the great space
behind was in vast expanses of richest purple gorgeous with heaven's
own perfect bloom.

If one were to characterize the district as 'a District of Surprises', I
think it would not be very difficult to justify the description. To any
one who may have studied the country in what may be termed the
physical geography way, but little in the way of justification would be
required. I remember a visit from one of the most accomplished men I
ever knew. He covered my dining-room table with the six-inch Ordnance maps of this part of the country. He spent the greater part of two
mornings in the diligent study of them, mastering all the details. And
at the end of the second morning he remarked, 'I have got it all in my
head now. To-morrow I shall go here and here and here' – indicating
three or four high points from which, it was clear from the maps, he
could get a very wide out-look – 'and survey the whole fashioning and
contour of all, and bring away a complete impression of the whole as a
mind-picture.'

I knew well enough what his thought and feeling and idea were, for I
had gone through the same process myself, only with worlds less of
geological knowledge; and, besides that, the mind-picture or plan of
this immediate portion of the district which he had thus worked out for
himself was but a part of the mind-picture or plan which I had once on
a time been aided to form with respect to the entire district of Cleve-

land. For I had seen, and been able to give some amount of attention to, a most carefully and accurately constructed model of the whole area named, planned and carried out on the scale and according to the lines of the Ordnance Survey. All was in proportion, the lengths and the breadths, the depths of the depressions, the elevations of the heights, the windings of the becks, the broader but hardly less tortuous wanderings of the rivers, every physical feature of the district lay there before me – on a small scale, it is true, but such and so true as to enable me easily to piece together such portions as I had been enabled to mark, study, and learn, according to the scale of Nature's own works.

And this helped me to realize how truly the district is one of surprises, and not only from the geographical point of view. To illustrate this. You toil up from the depths and gullies of Danby Head, and you find yourself with a wide sweep of moor in front, mounting still, on the whole. You trudge or toil, as the case may be, according as the ling is short or knee-deep and the walking easy or beset with damp and not wholly untreacherous places, and almost before you know or think about it, you find an enormous area for your eye to wander over. It is a clear day, and you see miles upon miles over the widening, lengthening prospect. You are ready to rub your eyes, and think they are playing you tricks. But it is York Minster you see, separated from you by only the small linear space of thirty-three miles or so. Wondering, you look on, and realize that the great pile lies there before you, like a huge ship at anchor on the surface, but not the extreme limit of the surface, of a great, smooth, still ocean. It is central on the sea, and not on the horizon. And the interpretation of that is, that you are looking over and beyond York and far into the more southerly distance.

Or you are a pilgrim and have been visiting the unsatisfactory shrine of the reputed British village, and have approached it from the Waupley side; and now you are breasting the ling-covered ascent between you and the Beacon – stopping for a moment, maybe, to note the stone which tells in simple words that there a man, lost and bewildered in a snowstorm, had been found dead, and shuddering a little perhaps at the thought of finding yourself in such case amid such a scene. And you climb up the last and steepest part of the hill, and mounting to the summit of the Beacon Hill – which has shut everything else out from your sight for the last twenty or twenty-five minutes – you pause and look round. And what a panorama it is that greets your eyes! Bold mountain ridge and coy shrinking dale from left to right as you face the south, and spreading round so as to overlap on the right side; and then turning seaward, the sea from Redcar Sands to almost Whitby, and right away out to the north the coast of Durham, beyond Sunderland and northward still, with an outline that seems to lose itself in the dim distance beyond. And a moment since you saw but a barren ling-covered moor-bank!

But to meet with surprises of the same class, it may be, but on a more limited and more appreciable, inasmuch as more familiar, scale, one should prowl about on the rough braes of the broken moor-banks, and within the romantic fastnesses of the Dales Heads. Every twenty yards almost, as you wind in and out, climb up or climb down, some new feature, some new object, some new scene, something you would give much to be able to photograph on the instant, and carry away with you indelible for ever, simply comes to be looked at; and as you turn aside, or press farther on in your course, gives way to another, equally beautiful and equally desirable in its beauty. In one word, our moorland scenery needs to be lived among.

It was the end of the season, and I wanted a few brace of grouse, which, if not shot that day, could be shot on no day at all. Certainly the moor was covered with snow; and getting near the birds under such circumstances was a matter of difficulty, and only to be thought of by one who did not mind walking in deep snow, and walking far and fast, – one well acquainted, moreover, not only with the moor itself, but with the haunts of the grouse at such times and under such circumstances. Well I knew every inch of the moor, and I did not mind walking it in snow; nor did I know what it was to get tired with even a long day's shooting. Besides, I had one of the under-keepers with me, who knew as well as I did the haunts of the birds, and all the bearings of the moor, and the different beats which might be taken with the especial object of circumventing the game[1] and getting a few shots from time to time within reasonable distance. Certainly the birds not only saw us as soon as we ascended to the moor-level, but flew off with more decisive promptitude than under ordinary circumstances at that time of year. But then we had this advantage too, that we could see them half a mile off, and even more than that when the packs were considerable; and

---

[1] This was many years before the modern system of driving had been so much as heard of. There is no difficulty now in getting birds if wanted; but thirty or forty years ago the case was very different.

we could see too whether there was any chance of a successful stalk of any of the packs within range of our eyesight. Suffice it to say that, sometimes by coming down upon them from above, and sometimes by surprising them from below, I got several shots, and very nearly the same number of grouse.

We had followed a lot which had sped their way from the higher part of the moor to a rather narrow tongue of moorland which stretched itself downwards in the direction of the part of the dale in which my house stands; and after another successful shot, we were about turning our steps in the direction of the higher moor, when all at once, for we seemed to have had no previous warning, we found ourselves in the midst of one of the thickest snowstorms I had ever experienced, even in these northern parts of the kingdom. Luckily it was not a 'hoddin' (holding or lasting) storm', for the snow ceased in less than half an hour; but it was succeeded, and as suddenly as it had burst upon us, by a fog so dense that we could not see ten yards in any direction – at times not ten feet. After a pause of a few minutes to see if the fog would lift in the same unforeseen and unaccountable way as the snow had come, had ceased, and been succeeded by the fog, I said to my companion, 'Well, William, I think we shall do no more good to-day'; his reply being, 'Neea, Ah aims it's overed for to-day'. And so we determined to set our faces homewards.

When this decision was taken we were on the eastern verge of a lofty but narrow ridge of moorland, the utmost transverse width of which at the point we stood on did not greatly exceed half a mile. Our object and intention was simply to cross it from east to west, and then to descend slopingly, so as to reach my home by the readiest way. Even if we had not been practised moorsmen, both of us, with a personal knowledge of every inch of the moor for miles away, we should have had no misgiving about the result. We had but to set our faces with our backs to the brae we stood upon, and keep on straight ahead, and fifteen minutes would take us to the point we meant to reach.

But we walked thirty minutes, and still no sign of the moor-edge we wanted to get to! At last the fog seemed to lift a little; and in a minute or two we saw it was because we were near the western edge of the ridge. But instead of being where we had intended to be, we were at least a mile farther up the ridge, and a good mile and a half from my house, instead of only three or four fields above it.

Laughing a little at our discomfiture, we proceeded to retrace our steps, having to go more out on to the moor in order to obtain a better trackway; for we thought that, where we were, it would be easy to skirt the moor-edge; and we had no idea but that we were skirting it as we continued our trudge. But when we next came to a point at which it was possible to recognize our landmarks, we found we had been traversing the ridge in a north-easterly direction, and had reached its verge a little above the hollow we call Coums!

Yet once more we addressed ourselves to what was proving to be rather a difficult task; and this time, when we came to the brae again, it was at a place not more than half a mile south of the intended point, and about less than a mile distant from the parsonage.

Now in the course of our vagaries we had crossed the Church-way twice, and another moor-road called the Mill-way four times, both of them tracks which had been worn down by weather and traffic to the depth of from a foot and a half to nearly three feet (in places) below the level of the moor, and along the side of each of which are set divers tall posts of unhewn stone to act as indications of the line of the said ways; but we had crossed them without knowing we were crossing, although of course, we had to plunge through the snow with which they were filled; and as to the guide-stones, unless we had almost run against them we could not have seen them for the fog. So that to all intents and purposes we experienced all the sensations of being lost, short only of the anxiety and the sense of peril from absolute ignorance alike of which way we ought to go and of the path we ought to select; and the experience was by no means a pleasant one.

Another case of 'Lost on the Moor', very much more real and actual than this, took place in the instance of two lads very well known to me. They were boys of twelve or thirteen years of age, and, as the custom was, and more then than now, they had gone out 'St. Thomasing', that is, visiting the farmhouses on St. Thomas's Day (20th December) and asking 'Thomas's gifts'. These were usually pieces of 'pepper-cake' (or the customary thick Christmas ginger-bread), with perhaps a modicum of cheese, or a bite of cake, or maybe a few halfpence. The day was dull and raw, but not bitterly cold. They had reached the farm called Stormy Hall, and then, finding the afternoon growing dark, and more thickness setting in, they made up their minds to give up for the day, and to turn their steps homewards the 'soonest way' they could go; and this was to leave the fringe of farmhouses that lie all along the dale just about the level of the highest enclosure, and the rough road that gives the means of going from one to the other all along, and making up the hill slopingly in order to reach the main road running along the top of the ridge from Kirkby Moorside to Castleton, where their parents lived. All this, however, was not made out until the next day, for the poor boys had never reached home. The anxiety of the parents – the boys were cousins – need not be dwelt upon.

It so happened the next morning that I had to take an early walk into the outlying part of the parish which Fryup is, and it was near midday when I returned to the Parsonage. Just before entering the garden from the Fryup side I heard a number of voices in the lane, and presently saw the speakers coming down the lane from the school. This was so unusual at the time named, for twelve o'clock is invariably called 'dinner-time', that I knew there must be some greatly exciting cause to account for this neglect of the midday meal; and instead of going into the house I went into the road to meet the men I had seen. Nearly the first person I met was a stalwart mason, then and always a great friend of mine, who told me that the two boys I have mentioned had never reached home, and to judge by the answers to inquiries made along the line they had taken the previous afternoon, they must have spent the night totally unsheltered on the open moor. My friend Frank's voice shook as he told me this. He was no ways related to the missing lads, but he was himself the father of lads of about the same age, and there was no lack of natural feeling about him. In fact he was a good fellow all round.

We organized our plan of search at once, and passing in loose order along the fields on the west side of the dale, we made towards the moor above Stormy Hall as directly as we could. We had not proceeded far before a shout came down the dale, and was passed on to us in the rear with a speed that seemed almost marvellous, to the effect that 'one of the lads had been found, and though very stiff and lame from the exposure, still not materially the worse.'

We soon met with further and fuller intelligence; and it appeared that the boys, bewildered by the fog, which they had found very dense as they ascended the moor-bank from the farm, and indeed increasing in thickness the higher they reached, had almost immediately, and in a way which they could not explain, gone astray from the right direction; and the deviation once made, although in the clear light it might seem to have been an unimportant one, yet, as always in a thick fog, it had the inevitable consequence of leading step by step to bewilderment. Our poor luckless little lads soon found they were out of

WINTER ON THE MOORS

the track, and effort after effort to recover it only ended in disappoint-
ment and hopeless discomfiture. And then the darkness of coming
night began to intensify the heavy gloom of the fog. But the brave,
hardy little chaps did not give up or lose either heart or head in their
trouble. They were lost, and they must spend the night on the open
moor. Well then, they must make the best of it, and do what they could
towards making the inevitable as bearable as they could. And so they
looked out a hollow way worn by the feet of sheep, and dry, and
sheltered by a growth of tall ling; and then they pulled some more ling
to hap themselves withal, and munching some of the gifts of food they
had got at the different farms they had visited, they prepared to spend
the night as comfortably as wet boots and stockings and damp clothes
would permit.

When the morning broke at last – and the nights are long indeed
towards the end of December, and even sometimes to those who have
more luxurious appointments than a down-pressing canopy of dull
grayish-white fog, with damp ling for coverlet, and moist shoes and
stockings, and clothes in general far from dry, for sheet and blanket –
only one of the two was capable of movement, and he stiffly and with
difficulty. But with an effort he 'got hissel' scratted oop', and began to
think what was best to be done. As he sat and thought as well as he
could, poor little chap, he fancied he heard the tinkle of a bell, and if so,
it would mean deliverance! It was no sheep-bell that, if a bell at all; but
it would be the bell of the leading horse of a 'draught' (team) and it
would lead him to the high road, if only he had strength and feet to
struggle so far.

A minute or two, and he is assured it is a bell; and then he hears the
driver speaking to his horses. Away he goes, hobbling as well as he
can; but the passage of the draught along the beaten road is faster than
his with his numbed feet over the hindering ling, and the sounds of the
rescue that might be are getting a little ahead of him. With a choking
sense of something nearer like despair than any yet, he musters all his
strength for a last yell, and luckily he is heard. It was time; for his
strength was spent, brave little fellow that he was! The driver, who was
making his early way to the Rosedale Head coal-pits, stopped his
draught, shouted in response, and presently had the poor, chilled,
foot-numbed, aching little waif safe in his arms, hoisted him into the
the waggon, covered him with the hay the horses were to have eaten
while taking in the intended load of coal, weighing it, paying for it, and

so forth, turned away straight back for Castleton, and dropped the rescued youngster at his father's door.

But the boy had not forgotten his fellow in the night's bivouac, who, moreover, as being less hardy than himself, was really and sadly disabled, but had given such an account of his own position when he first heard the sound of the bell, and of the way he had taken in trying to intercept the draught, that there was no difficulty for William Robinson, the rescuer, to give minute directions to such as he fell in with on the road how to look for the lost and helpless sojourner still left in his comfortless night's lodgings. And thus, before the party I had joined had had more than time to spread themselves out in a long line, each individual within hailing-distance, if not sight, of his right- and left-hand neighbours, and to begin the systematic search of every yard of the moor before us, the news came up from behind that the boy had been, found, had been taken down to Stormy Hall, and was there quite 'safe' though by no means 'sound'.

In half an hour's time the poor boy had more visitors than ever before or since in his life. We found him near a cheery farmhouse fire, were told he had enjoyed some warm milk, and, except that he had for the time lost the use of his legs and feet, did not seem to be materially the worse. The doctor too had seen him; for he had come riding up to join the army of seekers, and was on the spot almost as soon as wanted; and had said that he must stay where he was for a day or two, and then might be taken home without hurt; and that after a few days he would be as well again as ever.

But, thick as the fog was, there was more mist than could be accounted for on that ground in the eyes of more than one or two of the hardy rugged men who had joined in that search, when we realized what exposure on a North Yorkshire moorland in a December might must be, and did not as yet even fancy to ourselves that these strayed boys might have had coolness enough, and bravery besides, to try, hopeless as their case seemed, to do the best they could for themselves.

The brother of one of these boys paid me a visit only a few months ago. He had come home from one of the most distant of the English colonies to see the old place again, and he came to see his old friend the parson, and our talk fell on this episode among his early recollections; and we both of us seemed, at even such a long time after 'all had ended so well' to feel what a 'parlous' chance it was that his brother had passed through that night he was 'lost on the moor'.